THE BLOSSOM
COOKBOOK

THE BLOSSOM COOKBOOK

Classic Favorites from the Restaurant that Pioneered a New Vegan Cuisine

RONEN SERI • PAMELA ELIZABETH

CHEF RAMIRO RAMIREZ • ALEX ETLING

AVERY

an imprint of Penguin Random House

New York

AVERY

an imprint of Penguin Random House LLC
375 Hudson Street
New York, New York 10014

Most Avery books are available at special quantity discounts for bulk purchase for sales
promotions, premiums, fund-raising, and educational needs. Special books or book excerpts also
can be created to fit specific needs. For details, write SpecialMarkets@penguinrandomhouse.com.

Library of Congress Cataloging-in-Publication Data

Names: Seri, Ronen, author. | Elizabeth, Pamela, author. | Ramirez, Ramiro (Chef),
    author. | Etling, Alex, author.
Title: The Blossom cookbook : classic favorites from the restaurant that pioneered
    a new vegan cuisine / Ronen Seri, Pamela Elizabeth, Chef Ramiro
Ramirez, Alex Etling.
Identifiers: LCCN 2016057449 (print) | LCCN 2016058340 (ebook) | ISBN 9780399184888
    (hardcover : alk. paper) | ISBN 9780399184895 (ebook)
Subjects: LCSH: Vegan cooking. | LCGFT: Cookbooks.
Classification: LCC TX837 .S435 2017 (print) | LCC TX837 (ebook) | DDC 641.5/636—dc23
LC record available at https://lccn.loc.gov/2016057449
p.   cm.

Printed in the United States of America
10 9 8 7 6 5 4 3 2 1

Book design by Ashley Tucker

CONTENTS

My partner, Pamela Elizabeth, and I have been vegans since the mid '90s, when veganism was neither a common word nor a common lifestyle. What was more common was the notion that vegan food was bland, that it was a "radical" choice. At that time, there were very few vegan eateries in New York for us to dine in, let alone anything on the higher end. We could only order side dishes of vegetables and grains or be content to live on pasta while eating out. We saw an opportunity. As self-proclaimed foodies, we decided to open a restaurant that would allow us to offer people fine food, filled with flavor and richness, and also offer a cuisine free of cruelty to animals.

To open any restaurant is no easy task, and in a city like New York, where 80 percent of restaurants fail within the first five years, we were up for a challenging task. However, I truly believe that any business that is born from passion and

purpose, rather than just the bottom line, can generally stand the test of time. Blossom has been a testament to that belief.

It was only four months from the time Pamela and I had that first spark of an idea to the day we opened the doors at our first Blossom location. Situated in a turn-of-the-century historic duplex town house in the heart of Chelsea, the original Blossom began serving customers in 2005, and from those humble beginnings, I'm proud to say we have grown to be one of the premier vegan restaurants in the world, and we have succeeded in our original mission: to create a vegan cuisine for food lovers.

Before that first opening, our greatest challenge was finding the right chef. Vegan chefs were almost impossible to come by because there wasn't a developed vegan cuisine at the time. We were lucky to find a freelance chef who helped us create the foundation for our style of signature cooking. But since 2006, Chef Francisco (Ramiro Ramirez) has played the starring role in continuing to evolve our innovative menu. Chef Francisco joined as a young and eager prep cook after training under the supervision of top chefs at some of New York City's most prestigious restaurants. He was quickly able to beautifully translate our original mission to the plate, creating incredible vegan dishes that have kept Blossom a culinary destination

for vegans and vegetarians and anyone who loves inventive and delicious food.

At Blossom, we take our inspiration from world cuisine and remake traditional dishes, making sure the original spirit

of the dish is intact. Some of our most beloved menu items are elegant re-creations of comfort food using delicious—and healthy—replacements for meat. We love experimenting with seitan, tofu, and tempeh, marrying their hearty textures with classic techniques to create satisfying, rich meals. We also create unique dishes using fresh, seasonal vegetables that are healthier, whole, and balanced, without ever compromising on taste. These innovative dishes place vegetables front and center in a dish.

These days, the original Blossom and our second location on the Upper West Side are packed every night. We have also added a new location in the West Village and a sister group of takeout locations called Blossom du Jour.

I am proud to say that the Blossom of today is not viewed as a vegan restaurant, per se. We can easily say that more than 60 percent of our diners are nonvegan and simply love our food. Celebrities such as Ted Danson, Ethan Hawke, Alicia Silverstone, Woody Harrelson, Russell Simmons, and many others frequent our locations and our catering business is growing too. Business is thankfully continuing to *blossom*, and is booming.

Much has changed since we first opened our doors—interest in a vegan lifestyle has exploded and the best vegan chefs are reaching new heights. We are proud to have led the charge for more than ten years, showing skeptics that vegan food is every bit as rich, satisfying, and interesting as traditional food. We are lucky to see this revelation every day, in the eyes of a new "meat-loving" customer who can't believe our food can taste so delicious.

VEGAN FOR LIFE

My passion for veganism didn't start at an early age, and in some ways I experienced the transformation almost by chance. In 1997, I was on a silent meditation retreat in upstate New York. During the retreat, on a beautiful sunny September day, I was walking quietly by myself and noticed a sweet and rather large cow with a bell on her neck grazing in the field. She was so peaceful, so I came closer. She was watchful as I approached to make sure I was safe, and as I stood about six feet away, I felt her powerful quiet energy.

If you can live a life, enjoy great food, and be healthy without hurting another, why not do it?

We locked in a gaze and she had huge brown powerful eyes, and I immediately felt her depth and wisdom as she allowed me to look deep into her being. I know that it might sound strange, but I instantly knew right then and there that I would never eat meat again. My partner, Pamela, on the other hand, came to be a vegetarian at an early age after receiving a pamphlet in the mail from an animal sanctuary fund for animals that decreed the horrific practices of factory farming. Realizing the plight of animals for the first time, she went vegetarian on the spot, and vegan a few years later.

When people ask why I went vegan I always respond, *"If you can live a life, enjoy great food, and be healthy without hurting another, why not do it?"* Sometimes people are surprised to meet a six-foot-one athletic vegan man who loves food. To me, this is not a contradiction. I love eating plant-based, and I never feel hungry or deprived. Just the opposite! What's more, I have much more energy than when I ate a traditional diet. We only need to look to nature to prove that plant-based eating fuels our bodies—some of the most powerful animals are vegan: horses, zebras, giraffes, hippopotamuses, and more.

Today, people are learning about the health benefits of vegan food and experiencing them firsthand: the energy boost, clearer skin, digestive improvements, and healthy weight loss. Perhaps most important, more people

appreciate the benefits to the environment and enjoy the satisfaction of eating without cruelty. To Pamela and me, there is nothing more gratifying.

A NEW WORLD CUISINE

I grew up in Jerusalem, where so many people immigrated and literally brought their respective flavors from such countries as Morocco, Turkey, Yemen, Iran, Poland, Hungary, Spain, and Africa. It was an intoxicating place to learn about food, and unknowingly, I grew up with a very diverse palate. You'll find influences from these rich cuisines on our menu at Blossom. It's what has made us the gold standard of vegan fine dining. And these complex flavors are key to creating vegan dishes that vegans and nonvegans alike crave.

> It has been our greatest joy to see that everything we do can have a real impact on others and on the world around us.

If all the chefs of the world would put all their talent and skill into working only with vegetables and other vegan ingredients, can you imagine the food they would create? Not to mention the benefit to our health and environment. We would raise the overall consciousness of humanity by having an existence that is more compassionate in our world. Imagine a child growing up in a world where a cow, a pig, or a chicken is a playmate and not food. I truly see a deep connection between that and how we treat one another with a lot of the violence and unkindness that exists today.

A RECIPE FOR YOU . . . AND THE WORLD

I can't tell you how many people come to me and say that if they could eat Blossom's food every day, or could cook vegan dishes that would satisfy their significant others or children, they would do it. Well, now they can . . . and so can you! Over the years, both patrons and friends have been encouraging us to write a cookbook, and now we are delighted to finally share our trade secrets with you. These recipes are the product of years of experimentation and creativity. We hope these dishes will become staples in your home, too, and that you'll make them your own. We hope you'll enjoy our food and that you'll share it with others.

It has been our greatest joy to see that everything we do can have a real impact on others and on the world around us. One choice that Pamela and I made and acted on has now created a space and place for people to enjoy great food without the need to harm another. My hope is to keep that positive impact going and growing.

Thank you for supporting our mission and our part in evolving vegan cuisine. I hope you spend a lot of time in the kitchen with these recipes. And subscribe to our YouTube channel for our "How-To" series, where our cookbook comes to life!

With Utmost Sincerity,

Ronen Seri

SAUCES & DRESSINGS

PISTACHIO SAUCE

MAKES ABOUT 2 CUPS

We use this wonderful light-green sauce to finish our popular mushroom cigars (page 42). The gentle sweetness of the sauce balances the salty quality of the cigars. It's an ideal sauce for stronger, savory flavors, like dishes featuring mushrooms or other meat alternatives.

1 cup raw unsalted pistachios

1 tablespoon nutritional yeast

2 tablespoons extra-virgin olive oil

1 teaspoon salt

½ teaspoon black pepper

Put the pistachios, nutritional yeast, olive oil, salt, pepper, and 2 cups water in a high-speed blender. Blend until creamy. Adjust the consistency to your liking with more water, adding it 1 tablespoon at a time.

PISTACHIO PESTO

MAKES ABOUT 2 CUPS

Pistachios were a staple in my home growing up, so much so that my grandfather used to have them shipped all the way from Turkey! Why not create a cream sauce with them? Blended pistachios have a consistency that can make a wonderful cream substitute. When we swapped out pine nuts for the pistachios, it created such a creamy consistency that there was no need for cheese in our pesto sauce. Try it with ravioli or your favorite pasta.

3 bunches fresh basil

1 tablespoon chopped fresh garlic

½ cup raw unsalted pistachios

3 tablespoons extra-virgin olive oil

2 teaspoons salt

Bring a pot of water to a boil. Fill a medium bowl with ice and water and set it nearby. Blanch the basil leaves in the boiling water for 5 to 10 seconds to wilt them. Carefully remove the basil from the boiling water and submerge it in the ice water to stop the cooking process. Drain the basil, shaking off as much water as you can. Put the basil, garlic, pistachios, olive oil, salt, and ½ cup water in a high-speed blender and blend until smooth.

ALMOND-GINGER DRESSING

MAKES ABOUT 3 CUPS

A kale joy! Kale is a favorite of many because of its known health benefits and the antioxidants it contains. But it's also a little dry and can be tough. We created the delightful Almond-Ginger Dressing to make our kale salads mouthwatering and delicious—the citrus from the lemon juice and the healthy fats of the almonds help break down the tough fibers of the greens. Enjoy the smooth taste and light flavor with kale or other greens for beautiful summer and spring days.

1 cup almond butter, plus more if needed

½ cup maple syrup

½ cup fresh lemon juice

Zest of 1 lime

1 tablespoon chopped fresh ginger

Pinch of salt

Pinch of black pepper

Put the almond butter, maple syrup, lemon juice, lime zest, ginger, salt, pepper, and 1 cup water in a high-speed blender. Blend until smooth. Add more almond butter or water to achieve the desired consistency.

CAESAR DRESSING

MAKES ABOUT 1½ CUPS

We were certainly hesitant to give away the secret to our famous Caesar salad! We hear countless guests rave about our Caesar—no anchovies, Worcestershire sauce, or eggs necessary.

1 cup vegan mayonnaise, store-bought or homemade (page 27)

2 garlic cloves

1½ teaspoons Dijon mustard

1 tablespoon capers

1½ teaspoons nutritional yeast

Pinch of black pepper

Combine all the ingredients and ⅓ cup water in a high-speed blender. Blend until smooth.

RED WINE VINAIGRETTE

MAKES ABOUT 2¾ CUPS

This sweet and tangy dressing pairs well with lighter greens, like arugula. Make sure to use Dijon mustard, not yellow mustard.

1 cup red wine vinegar

2 tablespoons Dijon mustard

¼ cup finely minced shallots

¼ cup sugar

1 cup extra-virgin olive oil

In a medium bowl, whisk together the vinegar, mustard, shallots, and sugar. While whisking, stream in the oil and whisk until well combined and emulsified.

TAHINI DRESSING

MAKES ABOUT 1⅓ CUPS

Tahini is a fantastic ingredient in dressings, and more healthful than most people know! It contains a plethora of essential minerals like magnesium, copper, phosphorus, manganese, iron, and zinc. We use this tangy dressing on our famous Quinoa Salad (page 103).

¼ cup tahini

2 cloves fresh garlic

3 tablespoons fresh lemon juice

¼ cup extra-virgin olive oil

1 tablespoon salt

1 teaspoon pepper

Combine all the ingredients plus 1 cup water in a high-speed blender and blend until smooth.

CASHEW CHEESE

MAKES ABOUT 3½ CUPS

This is a simple, tangy, nut-based cheese. More complicated cheeses use cultures and probiotics, but this one is delicious, and considerably simpler to make. Enjoy it spread on your favorite crackers!

4 cups raw unsalted cashews

3 tablespoons tahini

¼ cup fresh lemon juice

¼ cup apple cider vinegar

1½ tablespoons salt

½ cup extra-virgin olive oil

Soak the cashews in cold water to cover in the refrigerator overnight. Drain the cashews and put them in a high-speed blender. Add the tahini, lemon juice, vinegar, salt, and oil. Blend until smooth.

| **NOTE:** You need to soak the cashews overnight, so be sure to plan ahead.

PARMESAN "CHEESE"

MAKES ABOUT 2 CUPS

Try this easy-to-make vegan Parmesan cheese on our pasta dishes or our Caesar salad.

1 cup raw unsalted almonds

1 cup nutritional yeast

½ teaspoon salt

Put the almonds in a food processor and process until finely ground. Add the nutritional yeast and salt and pulse until well combined.

TOFU RICOTTA

MAKES ABOUT 2½ CUPS

The light flavor of tofu is a fantastic substitute for lighter-flavored cheeses, like ricotta. The texture is spot-on! Try this ricotta in a vegan lasagna.

1 block firm tofu, drained

2½ tablespoons fresh lemon juice

2 tablespoons extra-virgin olive oil

2 tablespoons rice vinegar

2 teaspoons salt

½ teaspoon black pepper

Using your hands, crumble the tofu into a food processor. Add the lemon juice, olive oil, vinegar, salt, and pepper and pulse until well combined, but not smooth.

BLEU CHEESE SAUCE

MAKES ABOUT 1½ CUPS

Use this bleu cheese sauce to top our Buffalo Risotto Croquettes (page 38); it's also a great salad dressing or a dip for fresh crudités.

1 cup vegan mayonnaise, store-bought or homemade (page 27)

1 tablespoon finely chopped garlic

¼ cup finely chopped fresh parsley

¼ teaspoon salt

Pinch of black pepper

Combine all the ingredients in a high-speed blender and blend until smooth.

COCONUT CREAM

Coconut is an amazing substitute for heavy cream and other high-fat ingredients. In this recipe, coconut solids are whipped as you would heavy cream, with fantastically fluffy results. Top any pie with it, or simply spoon a bit over some fresh berries.

2 (14-ounce) cans full-fat coconut milk

2 cups confectioners' sugar

1 tablespoon vanilla extract

Chill the coconut milk can in your refrigerator overnight. The next day, carefully open the cans (do not shake) and pour off the clear liquid. Only the very thick white cream should remain. Put the contents of the cans, the confectioners' sugar, and the vanilla in a high-speed blender. Blend on low speed for 1 minute. Once the coconut and sugar are fully incorporated, increase the blender speed to high and blend for 3 to 4 minutes, until whipped.

I NOTE: You need to chill the coconut milk overnight, so be sure to plan ahead.

CASHEW CREAM

MAKES 6 TO 7 CUPS

With their high healthy-fat content, cashews are the best cream substitute, because when blended, they create an incredible richness for sauces. Who would ever think that an alfredo alternative could be so simple? One of our patrons' most frequently asked questions is "How do you do it?" when they eat our coveted fettuccine alfredo.

2 cups raw unsalted cashews, soaked for 3 hours or overnight

2 tablespoons nutritional yeast

3 tablespoons extra-virgin olive oil

1 tablespoon salt

1½ teaspoons black pepper

Drain the cashews and put them with the nutritional yeast, olive oil, salt, pepper, and 4 cups water in a high-speed blender. Blend until creamy. The sauce will be relatively thin, but will thicken quickly when heated in a recipe.

I NOTE: You need to soak the cashews 3 hours (or overnight), so be sure to plan ahead.

SOUR CREAM

MAKES ABOUT 2 CUPS

This is our favorite homemade vegan sour cream. The cashews add the healthy fat content, the tofu helps create the perfectly creamy texture, and the lemon juice adds that certain sour cream "tang." Try it on our Enchiladas (page 179).

2 cups raw unsalted cashews

⅓ cup fresh lemon juice

2 teaspoons salt

3 tablespoons olive oil

½ cup firm tofu, drained

Soak the cashews in cold water to cover in the refrigerator overnight. Drain the cashews and put them in a high-speed blender. Add the lemon juice, salt, olive oil, tofu, and ½ cup water. Blend until smooth.

VEGAN MAYONNAISE

MAKES ABOUT 2 CUPS

Who doesn't like mayonnaise? I find vegan versions even better than the original! So rich, creamy, and tasty. Cashews do the job of replacing eggs very well. Lemon juice, vinegar, and Dijon mustard give this mayo its distinctive tang. Use this recipe for any of our recipes that call for a mayo substitute, or as a finishing sauce or simple veggie dip!

1 cup raw unsalted cashews

1½ teaspoons fresh lemon juice

1 teaspoon brown rice syrup

1 teaspoon chopped garlic

2 teaspoons salt

2 teaspoons white wine vinegar

1 teaspoon Dijon mustard

1 cup extra-virgin olive oil

Soak the cashews in cold water to cover in the refrigerator overnight. Drain the cashews and put them in a high-speed blender. Add the lemon juice, brown rice syrup, garlic, salt, vinegar, mustard, olive oil, and ¼ cup water. Blend until creamy. Add more water as needed to reach the desired consistency.

| NOTE: You need to soak the cashews overnight, so be sure to plan ahead.

CHIPOTLE AIOLI

Mayonnaise is delicious, but sometimes you just need an extra kick of spice. That's where our famous Chipotle Aioli comes in. You can find this simple but tasty spread on many of our sandwiches. The chipotle peppers can be pretty fiery, so feel free to adjust the amount slightly to your spice preference.

2 cups vegan mayonnaise (page 27)

2 tablespoons canned chipotle peppers in adobo sauce

Put the vegan mayonnaise and chipotle peppers in adobo sauce in a high-speed blender. Blend until smooth.

HOLLANDAISE SAUCE

MAKES ABOUT 2½ CUPS

We use this rich hollandaise sauce on our Tofu Florentine (page 132). Everyone who tastes it inevitably asks how we can possibly make such a fantastic hollandaise without eggs. Now you know our secret!

1½ cups vegan mayonnaise, store-bought or homemade (page 27)

½ cup vegan butter, melted and kept warm

1 tablespoon fresh lemon juice

1 tablespoon Buffalo-style hot sauce

½ cup Cashew Cream (page 26)

1½ teaspoons ground turmeric

½ teaspoon black pepper

In a medium bowl, whisk together the vegan mayonnaise, vegan butter, lemon juice, hot sauce, cashew cream, turmeric, and pepper until fully combined and creamy. Gently warm in a small pan on the stovetop before serving.

AUTHENTIC GUACAMOLE

MAKES ABOUT 2 CUPS

There are two keys to making guacamole irresistibly delicious: You must use good, perfectly ripened avocados, and you must make your guacamole just before enjoying it. Fresh is best! This version is great served chunky and fantastic with fresh warm tortilla chips. Use a potato masher to get the perfect consistency!

4 ripe medium avocados, halved and pitted

¼ cup chopped fresh cilantro

2 tablespoons fresh lime juice

3 tablespoons chopped red onion

2 tablespoons chopped fresh jalapeño (optional)

1 teaspoon salt

½ teaspoon black pepper

Scoop out the avocado flesh into a medium bowl and mash with a potato masher or fork. Add the cilantro, lime juice, onion, jalapeño (if using), salt, and pepper and mash until the desired texture is reached. (We prefer ours a bit chunky.) Serve immediately.

CHIPOTLE TOMATILLO SALSA

MAKES ABOUT 4 CUPS

Tomatillos, also called Mexican husk tomatoes, don't get the respect they deserve! They're very culturally important in Mexican cuisine, dating back to the Mayan and Aztec civilizations. They make a great alternative to more common tomatoes when you are making salsa. The chipotle peppers in this recipe lend spice to this salsa—feel free to adjust the amount to suit your spice tolerance.

12 to 14 small to medium tomatillos

½ red onion, chopped

3 tablespoons canned chipotle peppers in adobo sauce

1 tablespoon salt

1 cup chopped fresh cilantro

Remove and discard the husks from the tomatillos. Wash the tomatillos well to remove any stickiness and dry them. Halve the tomatillos and put them in a high-speed blender. Add the onion, chipotle peppers in adobo sauce, salt, and 1 cup water. Blend until smooth, about 30 seconds. Add the cilantro and pulse until well combined.

MOLE

MAKES 4 TO 5 CUPS

Mole . . . peppered with flavor! In Mexico they take their mole seriously—very seriously. Having grown up in Mexico, Chef Francisco knows how to create the authentic taste of mole sauce, which uses three types of chile peppers: ancho, mulato, and pasilla peppers. You can find them dried in most grocery stores. The rich combination of these peppers makes this mole something truly special.

4 dried ancho chiles	½ medium Spanish onion	1½ teaspoons ground cumin
4 dried mulato peppers	4 garlic cloves	1½ teaspoons dried oregano
2 dried pasilla peppers	1 cup raisins	1½ tablespoons salt

Break off the ends of the ancho, mulato, and pasilla peppers and shake loose as many seeds as possible. Discard the seeds. Bring a large pot of water to a boil over high heat. Add the dried peppers to boiling water and boil for about 7 minutes, or until soft and rehydrated.

While the peppers are boiling, heat a medium skillet over medium-low heat. Add the onion, cut-side down, and garlic to the skillet and allow to gently blacken, about 3 to 5 minutes. Remove from the heat.

Drain the peppers and put them in a high-speed blender. Add the onion, garlic, raisins, cumin, oregano, salt, and 3 cups water. Blend until smooth. Pour the sauce into a medium saucepan and bring to a boil over high heat, then reduce the heat to medium and simmer for about 7 minutes.

MARINARA SAUCE

MAKES 5 TO 6 CUPS

While in Tuscany once, I visited a small family-owned Italian restaurant and tasted the best marinara sauce ever, on a bed of pasta with fresh basil. I approached Chef Francisco upon my return and asked him if he knew the secret to the coveted authentic red sauce. He did! His answer was simple, surprisingly simple, in fact. The keys to a wonderful marinara sauce are a very long cooking time, which reduces the acidity of the tomatoes, and a fresh pasta for serving. See for yourself—it's all in the simmer!

7 cups canned whole or crushed tomatoes

1½ tablespoons extra-virgin olive oil

1½ tablespoons minced garlic

1 cup chopped fresh basil

1 tablespoon sugar

⅛ cup salt

1 tablespoon black pepper

Put the tomatoes in a high-speed blender and blend until smooth.

In a large stockpot, heat the olive oil and garlic over medium-high heat. Sauté the garlic until it just begins to brown. Add the basil and sauté for 1 to 2 minutes. Add the blended tomatoes. Stir. Add the sugar, salt, pepper, and 6 cups water. Bring to a boil, then reduce heat to low and cook for 3 hours.

TANGY BBQ SAUCE

MAKES 8 TO 9 CUPS

This tangy BBQ sauce is the perfect complement to vegan proteins like tempeh and seitan—it's delicious on our BBQ Seitan Skewers (page 49). Every taste reminds us of summer cookouts—we'll admit to making our BBQ sauce in the middle of New York winters just to remind us of warmer weather!

½ medium onion, chopped

2 tablespoons chili powder

4 cups ketchup

1 cup molasses

1 cup apple cider vinegar

½ cup vegan Worcestershire sauce

¼ cup Dijon mustard

½ jalapeño

8 garlic cloves

In a medium stockpot, combine the onion, chili powder, ketchup, molasses, vinegar, Worcestershire sauce, mustard, jalapeño, garlic, and 1½ cups water and bring to a boil over high heat. Reduce the heat to medium and simmer for 5 to 10 minutes. Let cool, then transfer to a high-speed blender and blend until smooth.

APPETIZERS

One of our most popular menu items at Blossom, these crispy favorites became an instant hit. Best of all, they're easy to make, for fantastic hors d'oeuvres when entertaining or just as a delightful appetizer. The Buffalo-style hot sauce gives them a beautiful orange hue, as well as a distinct flavor.

BUFFALO RISOTTO CROQUETTES

Makes 12 to 16 balls

2 tablespoons extra-virgin olive oil

½ medium onion, finely diced

1½ cups Arborio rice

½ cup white wine

⅓ cup Buffalo-style hot sauce

1½ teaspoons salt

1 teaspoon black pepper

2 cups panko bread crumbs

Cooking oil

Bleu Cheese Sauce (page 24)

COOKING TIP: Ensure that the cooking oil is hot enough (350°F), or the risotto balls might fall apart.

1. In a medium pot, heat the olive oil over high heat. Add the onion and sauté for about 1 minute, until just translucent. Add the rice and white wine. Sauté for another minute. Add 2 cups water and bring to a boil, then reduce the heat to medium-low. Cover and simmer until water has been absorbed, 5 to 7 minutes.

2. Remove the rice mixture from the pot and let cool.

3. Place the cooled rice mixture in a large bowl and add the hot sauce, salt, and pepper. Mix well with your hands. Add ½ cup of the panko and continue to knead well with your hands. Form the mixture into golf-ball-size balls. Place the remaining panko in a small bowl. Roll the rice balls in the panko until well coated, pressing lightly if necessary to adhere.

4. In a deep skillet, heat 2 to 2½ inches (or enough to cover the croquettes) of cooking oil to 350°F. Working in batches of five or six, fry the croquettes for 4 to 5 minutes, until crispy and browned. Remove from the oil with a slotted spoon, and allow to drain briefly on a few folded paper towels on a large plate. Top with Bleu Cheese Sauce.

Pamela and I enjoy re-creating authentic cuisines from all over the world. Preparing and serving a variety of ethnic flavors allows us to share cultural interpretations of food. If I could pick a favorite cuisine, I would say Italian is what I enjoy most. I admire the way Italian chefs can create such incredible flavors and smells through combinations of herbs and sauces. We created these Seitan Meatballs to offer our patrons the enjoyment of eating "Mom's" traditional meatballs, with none of the animal products.

SEITAN MEATBALLS

Makes about 20 meatballs

½ medium onion, chopped

2 cups rolled oats (not instant)

4 cups very finely minced seitan

½ cup extra-virgin olive oil, plus more as needed

1 tablespoon garlic powder

½ cup Parmesan "Cheese" (page 23)

¼ cup chopped fresh parsley

1 tablespoon salt

1½ teaspoons black pepper

1. Preheat the oven to 350°F. Oil two baking sheets with a drizzle of olive oil.

2. In a large bowl, combine the onion, oats, seitan, olive oil, and garlic powder. Mix well with your hands until well combined. Spread the mixture over one prepared baking sheet. Bake for 15 to 20 minutes, or until the mixture begins to crisp and brown on top. Remove from the oven and let cool for 5 minutes; keep the oven on.

3. Transfer the mixture back to the bowl, and add the Parmesan, parsley, salt, and pepper and mix, using your hands if the mixture has cooled sufficiently. Add 1 to 2 tablespoons more olive oil, if necessary, to help the mixture stick together. At this point, the balls should hold their shape easily without falling apart. Roll the mixture into golf ball–size balls with your hands, and place the balls on the second prepared baking sheet. Drizzle the meatballs with olive oil and bake for 5 to 10 minutes, or until they begin to slightly crisp on the edges.

Porcini mushrooms are the star ingredient here, and their savory, umami-filled flavor shines next to the delicate crispiness of the rolled phyllo dough. What really brings this dish together is the Pistachio Sauce. Try not licking the plate—we dare you!

PORCINI PHYLLO CIGARS

Makes about 24 pieces

2 pounds fresh porcini mushrooms (20 to 24 mushrooms)

1 tablespoon crushed garlic

4 tablespoons extra-virgin olive oil

1 cup raw unsalted almonds

1 teaspoon salt

½ teaspoon black pepper

1 tablespoon truffle oil

1 (16-ounce) package phyllo dough

2 tablespoons vegan butter, melted

Pistachio Sauce (page 20)

1. Preheat the oven to 350°F. Oil a baking sheet with a drizzle of olive oil.

2. In a large bowl, combine the mushrooms, garlic, and olive oil and toss until the mushrooms are well coated. Spread the mushrooms onto the prepared baking sheet and bake for 15 to 20 minutes, or until they begin to shrivel and soften. Remove the mushrooms from the oven and transfer them to a food processor. Add the almonds, salt, pepper, and truffle oil and process until pureed.

3. Spread out a sheet of phyllo dough. With a pastry brush, brush melted vegan butter evenly over the sheet and then place another sheet on top. Repeat until you have a 3-sheet stack with vegan butter lightly brushed between layers. Spread a finger-size amount of the porcini mixture along one long end of the phyllo stack. Starting from the side containing the mushroom mixture, begin rolling up the phyllo into a long cylinder. Seal the edge with melted butter. Cut the cylinder crosswise into 6-inch sections. Repeat with the remaining phyllo, vegan butter, and mushroom filling.

RECIPE CONTINUES

4. In a large skillet, heat the olive oil over medium-high heat. Working in batches to avoid overcrowding the pan, place the phyllo cigars in the oil and cook, turning them as needed, until they are golden brown on all sides, 1 to 2 minutes per side. Serve with Pistachio Sauce.

When we opened our first location, Blossom in Chelsea, we consulted with an expert chef who helped create our first recipes. He was a lover of the spices of Sri Lanka and India, and this dish was one of his wonderful inventions. It was originally served with caramelized onions on top, but Chef Francisco and I later modified it by topping it with our Tofu Ricotta. The crispy, slightly sweet phyllo dough contrasts perfectly with the flavorful curry and cilantro, which truly makes the flavors pop. Serve it as an hors d'oeuvre, an appetizer, or a side to a main course. A wonderful winter dish to enjoy.

CURRIED LENTIL RINGS

Serves 4

2 cups dry French lentils

3 tablespoons extra-virgin olive oil

1 carrot, chopped

2 red bell peppers, diced

1 onion, chopped

½ cup chopped scallions

1 cup chopped fresh cilantro, chopped

1 teaspoon curry powder

1 teaspoon garlic powder

1 tablespoon salt, plus a pinch

Pinch of black pepper

1 (16-ounce) package phyllo dough

2 tablespoon vegan butter, melted

Tofu Ricotta (page 24)

1. Put the dry lentils in a large pot and add enough water to cover them. Bring to a boil over high heat. Reduce the heat to medium and simmer until the lentils are soft, about 30 minutes, then set aside.

2. In a medium skillet, heat 2 tablespoons of the olive oil over high heat. Add the carrot, bell peppers, and onion and sauté for 1 to 2 minutes, then reduce the heat to medium and sauté for 5 to 7 minutes more, or until the vegetables begin to soften. Set aside to cool.

3. In a large bowl, combine the lentils, carrot, peppers, onion, scallions, and cilantro. Stir well to combine. Add the curry powder, garlic powder, salt, and black pepper and mix until the spices are fully incorporated.

4. Spread out a sheet of phyllo dough. With a pastry brush, brush melted vegan butter evenly over the sheet and then

RECIPE CONTINUES

place another sheet on top. Repeat until you have a 4-sheet stack with vegan butter lightly brushed between layers. Spread the lentil mixture in a line about 1½ inches wide at one of the long ends of the phyllo stack. Starting from the side containing the lentil mixture, begin rolling up the phyllo into a long cylinder. Seal the edge with melted butter. Slice the cylinder crosswise into 6-inch sections.

5. In the skillet you used for the vegetables, heat the remaining 1 tablespoon olive oil over high heat. Place the phyllo rolls in the pan and fry until the rolls begin to crisp and brown. Brown on all sides, using caution when flipping and rolling, as phyllo dough is very delicate. Slice each roll in half on an angle and serve with Tofu Ricotta.

A summer classic, this dish was first introduced at our second location, Café Blossom. These are great to make at a backyard barbecue—an outdoor grill gives them an extra-smoky flavor.

BBQ SEITAN SKEWERS

Makes 6 to 8 skewers

1 pound seitan, cut into 1-inch cubes

2 cups Tangy BBQ Sauce (page 35)

1 tablespoon olive oil

1. Soak 6 to 8 wooden skewers in water for 30 minutes to prevent burning.

2. Thread the seitan cubes on the skewers. Put the BBQ sauce in a shallow bowl and dredge the skewers through the sauce, taking care to coat them thoroughly. Allow the skewers to marinate, refrigerated, up to 5 hours or overnight, if desired, for deeper flavor.

3. In a large skillet, heat the olive oil over medium heat. Add the skewers and sauté for 1 to 2 minutes. Add a splash of water and cover. Cook for 5 minutes, covered, or until heated through.

NOTE: After marinating, you can cook the skewers on a hot grill for 2 to 3 minutes, turning periodically, instead of on the stovetop. Serve two skewers per person.

This simple and wonderful seasonal dish came together while I was visiting a friend in East Hampton, New York. Driving back from the beach, I picked up fresh vegetables at an organic farm stand in Sagaponack. As I unpacked the most beautiful zucchini and tomatoes I had ever seen, my chef friend joked that we should make a tower out of the vegetables. We grilled the tomatoes and zucchini, and using pesto as our "mortar," created our Zucchini Napoleon—a petite tower with giant taste! If you can find heirloom tomatoes, the flavor will be even better.

ZUCCHINI NAPOLEON

Serves 3 as a small appetizer

1 medium to large zucchini

1 large tomato

Salt and black pepper

3 tablespoons olive oil

½ cup Pistachio Pesto
  (page 20)

1. Cut the zucchini in half crosswise, then cut each half lengthwise into ¼-inch-thick slices. Slice the tomato into ¼-inch-thick slices, then halve the tomato slices. Sprinkle both sides of the zucchini and tomato slices with a pinch each of salt and pepper. Drizzle with 2 tablespoons of the olive oil.

2. In a large skillet, heat the remaining 1 tablespoon olive oil over medium-high heat. Add the zucchini slices and sauté, flipping them as needed until they begin to brown on each side and become slightly soft. Remove the zucchini and set aside. Add the tomato slices to the pan and sauté for 1 to 2 minutes.

3. Spread a small amount of pesto on each plate, followed by a slice of zucchini, additional pesto, and a slice of tomato. Repeat the layers to the desired height.

These little crispy tempeh balls are the perfect substitute to the Seitan Meatballs if you are looking for a different flavor or would simply prefer a gluten-free option. We created these at our Chelsea location and serve them as hors d'oeuvres, but feel free to enjoy them with your favorite gluten-free pasta for a wonderful, hearty meal. Top with a fine olive oil or our Marinara Sauce (page 33).

CRISPY TEMPEH BALLS

Makes 15 or 16 balls

4 celery stalks, chopped

1 large carrot, diced

1 (8-ounce) package tempeh

½ medium onion, chopped

1½ teaspoons chopped garlic

3 tablespoons extra-virgin olive oil

1 tablespoon salt

1½ teaspoons black pepper

2 cups panko bread crumbs

2 cups cooking oil (we recommend grapeseed, safflower, or sunflower)

1. Preheat the oven to 350°F. Add the celery and carrot to a large mixing bowl. Using your hands, crumble the tempeh into the bowl. Add the onion, garlic, olive oil, salt, and pepper. Spread the mixture onto a baking sheet, and bake for 10 to 15 minutes.

2. Remove the mixture from the oven, and add to a food processor. Process until ground finely. Place the mixture into a large bowl, and roll into golf ball–sized balls with your hands. Add the panko bread crumbs to a large bowl. Dredge the tempeh balls in panko, and set aside. Add the cooking oil to a large skillet on medium-high heat. Pan-fry the tempeh balls for 2 to 3 minutes, or until golden brown.

NOTE: After frying, you can bake the tempeh balls for 7 to 10 minutes in the oven at 350°F to make them extra crispy.

Watching the NBA Playoffs with friends at a random bar in New York City, I observed the majority of the crowd ordering calamari. It was that night that I thought, "Why not make a vegan calamari?!" Amazingly, trumpet mushrooms perfectly mimic the texture of calamari. Serve with Marinara Sauce and a fresh lemon wedge on the side for the full effect. Enjoy the game!

TRUMPET MUSHROOM CALAMARI

Serves 3 or 4

4 large king trumpet mushrooms

3 tablespoons tamari or soy sauce

1 cup cornmeal

1 cup all-purpose flour

2 tablespoons chili powder

2 tablespoons paprika

2 tablespoons onion powder

2 tablespoons garlic powder

1 cup chopped fresh basil

1 tablespoon salt

1½ teaspoons black pepper

4 cups grapeseed, safflower, or sunflower oil

Marinara Sauce (page 33)

1. Slice off the tops and bottoms of the mushrooms. Cut them into ½-inch-thick slices. (Optional step: Use an apple corer or similar kitchen tool to remove the center of each mushroom slice.) Add the finished slices to a large mixing bowl, and add 10 cups water and the tamari. Marinate for 3 to 5 hours, or overnight in the refrigerator.

2. Add the cornmeal, flour, chili powder, paprika, onion powder, garlic powder, basil, salt, and pepper to a large mixing bowl. Drain the mushrooms, and dredge in the breading mixture, using your hands to fully coat each mushroom slice.

3. Add the cooking oil to a deep skillet, and heat on medium-high heat until the oil begins to bubble. Add the mushroom slices and fry for about 7 minutes, or until they are golden brown. Remove from the oil and serve with Marinara Sauce.

This is Blossom's signature appetizer, and one of the dishes we first served at our original Chelsea location. A fantastic Sri Lankan–influenced dish, it has since become a staple; we couldn't take it off the menu even if we wanted to! It's easy to make these cakes whatever size you'd like—smaller cakes make great hors d'oeuvres, or make larger cakes for a meal.

BLACK-EYED PEA CAKES

Makes about 4 large or 8 small cakes

6 medium Yukon Gold potatoes

⅓ cup dried black-eyed peas

2 tablespoons olive oil

1 red bell pepper, finely chopped

1 medium red onion, finely chopped

2 tablespoons chopped fresh cilantro

2 tablespoons chopped scallions

1 teaspoon garlic powder

1 teaspoon curry powder

1 teaspoon salt

½ teaspoon black pepper

2 cups panko bread crumbs

Cooking oil (we recommend grapeseed, safflower, or sunflower)

Chipotle Aioli (page 29)

1. Bring a large pot of water to a boil. Add the whole potatoes, skins on, and boil for about 35 minutes, or until soft. While the potatoes are boiling, bring a slightly smaller pot of water to a boil, add the black-eyed peas, and boil for 25 to 30 minutes, or until soft. Remove the potatoes from the water, and mash in a large mixing bowl, leaving the skins on. Allow to cool.

2. Heat the olive oil in a large skillet on medium-high heat; add the peppers and the onions. Sauté for about 5 minutes, or until soft. Remove from heat and allow to cool. Add the black-eyed peas, peppers, onions, cilantro, scallions, garlic, curry, salt, and pepper to the mashed potatoes, and mix well, using your hands or a handheld mixer. Form the mixture into golf ball–sized balls using your hands. Dredge the balls in panko bread crumbs, turning until well-coated. Fill a deep skillet 2 inches deep with cooking oil, or enough to cover pea cakes, and heat to 350°F. Fry the pea cakes for about 3 minutes, or until golden brown and crispy. Remove from the oil, and serve with our Chipotle Aioli.

Invented by a guest chef for a Valentine's Day menu, this savory and sweet dish is a celebration of the senses. We love the contrast between the sweetness of the parsnips and the saltiness of the crispy mushrooms on top, as well as the deep flavors of the sage and truffle. We had a very hard time taking this dish off the menu, so it reappears frequently as a special.

PARSNIP RAVIOLI

Makes 12 ravioli

3 medium parsnips, chopped in 2-inch pieces

1 cup semolina wheat flour

1 cup all-purpose flour, plus more for rolling

1½ teaspoons salt

Pinch of black pepper

3 tablespoons truffle oil

2 tablespoons olive oil

1 cup chopped shiitake mushrooms

2 tablespoons vegan butter

1 tablespoon chopped fresh sage

1. Bring a large pot of water to a boil. Add the chopped parsnips and boil until soft, 30 to 40 minutes.

2. While the parsnips boil, add the semolina and all-purpose flours to a large mixing bowl. Add ¾ cup water very slowly, kneading with your hands while incorporating the water, until the dough is fully combined and easy to work with.

3. Once the parsnips are soft, remove them from the water and place in a food processor. Add the salt, pepper, and 2 tablespoons truffle oil. Process the parsnips until smooth.

4. Separate the dough into two equal parts. On a well-floured surface, roll both dough sections with a rolling pin until about ⅛ inch thick. Once the dough is rolled out, slice it into even strips about 3 inches wide. Spoon 1½ tablespoons of the parsnip mix in dollops on one side of half of the strips of dough, spacing each dollop out about 3 fingers from the nearest one. Lay the other sheet of dough on top, and use your fingers to push out the air, sealing around each dollop with your fingers. Using a cookie cutter, cut out the raviolis. You should have about 12 ravioli.

RECIPE CONTINUES

5. Bring a large pot of water to a boil. Add the ravioli and boil until soft, about 7 minutes. Remove from water; set aside. Add 2 tablespoons of olive oil to a skillet on medium-high heat. Add the shiitakes, and sauté until browned. Set aside. Add the vegan butter to a skillet on medium-high heat. Add the cooked ravioli, 1 tablespoon truffle oil, and the sage. Sauté the ravioli for 1 to 2 minutes.

6. Plate 3 ravioli per serving, and top with the shiitakes.

Mushrooms are one of our favorite ingredients, as their diversity in size, taste, and texture allows us to experiment and get very creative with our interpretations of traditional dishes. In this dish, we use king trumpet mushroom to mimic the flavors and luxurious texture of scallops. It works perfectly! What makes this appetizer so special is that you can play with different seasonal sauce ideas. For example, the porcini sauce with rich polenta makes a wonderful fall or winter dish, while a cream sauce and a dash of vegan Parmesan cheese make a fantastic summer dish. Originally introduced as one of our first "in bloom" creations, Trumpet Mushroom Scallops quickly became one of our most popular and loved dishes.

TRUMPET MUSHROOM SCALLOPS

Serves 2

FOR THE MUSHROOM MARINADE AND STOCK

1 large king trumpet mushroom (as thick as possible)

1 tablespoon chopped garlic

1 tablespoon chopped shallots

1½ teaspoons salt, plus more as needed

Pinch of black pepper, plus more as needed

FOR THE POLENTA

½ cup Cashew Cream (see page 26)

1½ teaspoons finely chopped shallots

1½ teaspoons finely chopped garlic

1. Make the mushroom marinade and stock: Slice the trumpet mushrooms into 1-inch slices. In a high-speed blender, combine 2⅓ cups water, the garlic, shallots, salt, and pepper and blend until smooth. Pour the marinade into a large bowl or container and add the trumpet mushrooms. Marinate the mushrooms in the refrigerator for 5 hours or overnight.

2. Make the polenta: In a medium pot, combine the Cashew Cream, shallots, garlic, salt, vegan butter, and 1 cup water and bring to a boil over high heat. Add the polenta gradually, stirring continuously for 1 to 2 minutes, until the water is absorbed, then remove from the heat. Set aside.

3. Make the porcini sauce: Bring 2 cups water to a boil in a small pot and then remove from heat. Add the dried porcini mushrooms. Let soak for at least 1 hour. Remove

RECIPE CONTINUES

1 teaspoon salt

1 tablespoon vegan butter

½ cup polenta

FOR THE PORCINI SAUCE

1 cup dried porcini mushrooms

2 tablespoons olive oil

1 tablespoon finely chopped
    shallots

3 tablespoons white wine

1 tablespoon vegan butter

Pinch of salt

Pinch of black pepper

FOR THE SPINACH

1 tablespoon olive oil

1 tablespoon finely chopped
    garlic

1 handful spinach

Pinch of salt

2 tablespoons olive oil

the rehydrated mushrooms from the water, set the soaking water aside, and discard the mushrooms or use them in another recipe.

4. In a medium skillet, heat the olive oil over high heat. Add the shallots and sauté for 1 to 2 minutes. Add the white wine (be careful—it may flame up) and sauté for 1 minute. Add the porcini soaking liquid, the vegan butter, the salt, and the pepper. Simmer until the sauce has reduced, then set aside.

5. Make the spinach: In a separate medium skillet, heat the olive oil over medium-high heat. Add the garlic and sauté for 1 to 2 minutes, then add the spinach and salt. Sauté for 1 to 2 minutes, or until spinach is fully cooked. Set aside.

6. Remove the trumpet mushrooms from the marinade and sprinkle with a pinch each of salt and pepper. In a skillet, heat the olive oil over medium heat. Add the trumpet mushrooms and cook for 1 to 2 minutes on each side, until beginning to brown.

7. To serve, divide the polenta between two plates, followed by the spinach, then the trumpet mushroom scallops. Finish with the porcini sauce. Enjoy!

Who doesn't love tacos? While mushrooms are the main ingredient in this recipe, the authentic Mexican sauce, using traditional guajillo chiles, is what really makes the flavors in this dish pop. You can find these mildly spicy peppers in dried form in most supermarkets, or your local Mexican market. We love to serve them in a small trio with a lime wedge on the side, and a bottle of hot sauce at the ready!

ADOBO MUSHROOM TACOS

Serves 2 or 3; makes 6 small tacos

10 dried guajillo chiles

1 tablespoon canned chipotle peppers in adobo sauce

2 cups canned whole tomatoes

1½ teaspoons oregano

2 tablespoons apple cider vinegar

½ medium onion

2 tablespoons chopped garlic

2 tablespoons salt, plus a pinch

3 tablespoons olive oil

5 cups sliced white button mushrooms

Pinch of black pepper

Six 5-inch corn tortillas

Shredded cabbage or lettuce, for serving

Chipotle Tomatillo Salsa (page 30) or your favorite salsa

1. Remove the stems from the guajillo chiles and pour out dried seeds. Place the chiles in a large pot. Add the chipotle peppers in adobo, tomatoes, oregano, vinegar, onion, 1 tablespoon of the garlic, 2 tablespoons salt, and 4 cups water. Bring to a boil over high heat and cook until the dried chiles become soft, 20 to 25 minutes. Once the peppers are soft, transfer the contents of the pot to a high-speed blender and blend until smooth. Set aside.

2. In a large skillet, heat 2 tablespoons of the olive oil over high heat. Add the remaining 1 tablespoon garlic and sauté for 1 minute, then add the mushrooms and a pinch each of salt and black pepper. Sauté for 1 to 2 minutes, then reduce the heat to medium and sauté until the mushrooms are soft and slightly browned (about 5 minutes). Remove from heat and set aside.

RECIPE CONTINUES

Sour Cream (page 27)

Other toppings of your choice

3. In a large pot, heat the remaining 1 tablespoon olive oil over high heat. Add the guajillo sauce and bring to a boil, then reduce the heat to medium and simmer for about 4 minutes. Add the sauce to the skillet with the mushrooms and stir well.

4. Spoon the finished Adobo Mushrooms onto a tortilla and garnish with lettuce, salsa, vegan sour cream, and your favorite toppings.

When I was a child in Israel, deviled eggs were served as appetizers at weddings. I distinctly remember my father shooting me a look, as if to say, "Don't eat so many this time!" When I was working with Chef Francisco on Blossom's seasonal "in bloom" menu, he suggested deviled eggs. I agreed enthusiastically, but never dreamed that a vegan version would be so good. The combination of chickpeas, mustard, and turmeric perfectly replicates the taste and texture of the yolks, while the marinated tofu is a perfect stand-in for egg whites. So innovative and delicious! To serve this dish as a more elegant appetizer, include the optional parsnip sauce. Don't forget to top with a dash of paprika.

DEVILED "EGGS"

Serves 4; makes about 12 "eggs"

FOR THE "EGG WHITES"

1 (14-ounce) block firm tofu, drained

2 tablespoons apple cider vinegar

FOR THE "EGG YOLKS"

2 (14-ounce) cans chickpeas, drained and rinsed

4 tablespoons vegan mayonnaise, store-bought or homemade (page 27)

1 tablespoon yellow mustard

1½ teaspoons paprika

1½ teaspoons ground turmeric

1 teaspoon fresh lemon juice

1½ teaspoons salt

1. **Make the "egg whites":** Bring a medium pot of water to a boil. Cut the tofu lengthwise into three even slices. Add the vinegar to the boiling water, then add the tofu and boil for 3 minutes. Remove from the water and let cool for a minute or two. Cut the tofu slices into egg-shaped ovals— you should be able to cut four "eggs" out of each slice of tofu. Place the tofu in the refrigerator to cool.

2. **Make the "egg yolks":** Bring a medium pot of water to a boil. Add the chickpeas and boil until very soft, 8 to 10 minutes (this helps create the yolklike texture of the filling). Drain the chickpeas and transfer to a high-speed blender. Blend until smooth. If the chickpeas are not smooth, feel free to add small amounts of water until you achieve a yolklike consistency. Add the vegan mayonnaise, mustard, paprika, turmeric, lemon juice, salt, and pepper.

RECIPE CONTINUES

¼ teaspoon black pepper

3 tablespoons chopped fresh
chives

Paprika, for serving

FOR THE PARSNIP SAUCE
(OPTIONAL)

1 tablespoon extra-virgin
olive oil

4 parsnips, cubed

1 medium onion, chopped

1 (14-ounce) can coconut milk

1 tablespoon ground turmeric

1 tablespoon nutritional yeast

Salt and black pepper

Blend again to combine. Transfer the "yolk" mixture to a bowl and gently stir in the chives. Chill the chickpea "yolk" in the refrigerator, if desired.

3. To assemble, dollop some "egg yolk" on top of each "egg white." Sprinkle with paprika and enjoy!

FOR THE PARSNIP SAUCE (OPTIONAL)

4. In a medium pot, heat the olive oil over medium-high heat. Add the parsnips and onion and sauté for 1 to 2 minutes. Add the coconut milk, turmeric, nutritional yeast, 1 cup water, and salt and pepper to taste. Cook until the parsnips are soft, about 7 minutes. Transfer the mixture to a high-speed blender and blend until smooth.

5. Divide the sauce among four plates and top with the "eggs."

As someone who grew up in Jerusalem, I can assure you that I know and appreciate great hummus. The difference between great hummus, good hummus, and bad hummus is huge! This easy-to-make hummus was originally inspired by a Turkish friend of mine; it tastes authentic, without taking hours to make. The blending time is not a mistake; it needs time to get exceptionally smooth and creamy, which is part of what elevates this hummus. Try it! It will surprise you. Top with a drizzle of high-quality olive oil and serve with fresh pita.

AUTHENTIC HUMMUS

Makes 4 to 5 cups

3 cups cooked chickpeas

1 cup extra-virgin olive oil

¼ cup tahini

1 teaspoon ground cumin

1½ tablespoons fresh lemon juice

2 garlic cloves

1 teaspoon salt

½ teaspoon black pepper

Put all the ingredients in a high-speed blender and add ½ cup water. Blend for 10 to 15 minutes, or until very, very smooth.

SIDE DISHES

Perfectly cooked Brussels sprouts aren't always easy to achieve. Many times, the outside will be nice and crispy while the inside is still tough. The combination of sautéing and then oven roasting will ensure your Brussels sprouts are perfect through and through.

BRUSSELS SPROUTS

Serves 1 (easily multiplied)

1 tablespoon extra-virgin olive oil

1½ teaspoons minced fresh garlic

1 cup Brussels sprouts, halved

Salt and black pepper

1. Preheat the oven to 350°F.

2. In a medium skillet, heat the olive oil over medium-high heat. Add the garlic and sauté for a minute or two, until just starting to brown. Add the Brussels sprouts and sauté for 1 minute. Season with salt and pepper. Add a small amount (1 to 2 tablespoons) of water to the pan to soften the sprouts. Spread the Brussels sprouts over a baking sheet (or keep in the skillet if it is oven-safe) and roast until soft and beginning to brown, about 7 minutes.

This is a simple but beautiful side dish. The blended cilantro perfectly coats each grain of rice, creating a gorgeous green dish that is absolutely packed with flavor. We like to serve this as a side for our Poblano en Nogada (page 175) because the cilantro balances the sweetness of the fruit in the stuffed pepper.

CILANTRO RICE

Makes about 3 cups

2 tablespoons olive oil

1 cup jasmine or basmati rice

1½ teaspoons salt

2 cups chopped fresh cilantro

Zest and juice of 1 lime

1. In a medium pot, heat the olive oil over high heat. Add the rice and sauté, stirring, for 1 to 2 minutes. Add 2 cups water and the salt, bring to a boil, then reduce the heat to medium and cover. Once the water has been absorbed, about 7 minutes, remove from the heat and let rest, still covered, for 5 to 10 minutes.

2. Fill a medium bowl with ice and water. Bring a small pot of water to a boil. Blanch the cilantro in the boiling water for 30 seconds, then transfer to the ice water. Let cool for 1 to 2 minutes, then drain and transfer the cilantro to a high-speed blender. Blend until smooth, adding small amounts of water as needed to encourage blending.

3. Stir the blended cilantro, lime zest, and lime juice into the rice until well combined, and serve.

Kale and squash make a fantastic veggie combo. Butternut squash is naturally sweet, which balances the light bitterness of the kale. Add just a touch of garlic, salt, and pepper, and you've got a perfectly simple side dish.

SAUTÉED KALE AND BUTTERNUT SQUASH

Serves 4

½ medium butternut squash, peeled, seeded, and cut into 1-inch cubes

4 tablespoons extra-virgin olive oil

1½ tablespoons minced garlic

½ teaspoon salt, plus a pinch

2 pinches of black pepper

2 bunches kale, torn into small pieces

1. Preheat the oven to 350°F.

2. In a bowl, combine the squash, 2 tablespoons of the olive oil, 1 tablespoon of the garlic, ½ teaspoon of the salt, and a pinch of pepper and toss gently to coat the squash cubes. Spread over a baking sheet, cover with aluminum foil, and roast for 15 minutes, or until soft.

3. In a large skillet, heat the remaining 2 tablespoons olive oil. Add the remaining ½ tablespoon garlic to the pan and sauté for 30 seconds. Add the kale and sauté for 1 minute. Add the butternut squash and a pinch each of salt and pepper. Sauté until soft, about 2 minutes.

While we love creating inventive recipes with tofu like our Pistachio-Crusted Tofu (page 161), or using it to create dips and sauces, sometimes some simply prepared tofu is just what you need. We love to add this perfectly prepared tofu to salads for an extra protein kick.

PAN-FRIED TOFU

Makes 8 slices

1 (14-ounce) package extra-firm tofu, drained and gently pressed between paper towels

2 tablespoons extra-virgin olive oil

1½ teaspoons minced garlic

1½ teaspoons tamari

1. Slice the tofu along the longest edge into four even slices. Cut each slice diagonally to create eight triangular slices.

2. In a large skillet, heat the olive oil over medium-high heat. Add the garlic and sauté until it just begins to brown, 1 to 2 minutes. Add the tofu and sauté for 1 minute, then flip and sauté for another minute. Add the tamari and 1 cup water. Sauté for 2 minutes more. Remove from the heat and serve.

This dish is inspired by traditional Kurdish cuisine, which we were introduced to by our neighbor and friend Azman. Quinoa is a particularly rich source of vegan protein, but it's not very flavorful on its own. This preparation gives it a delicious, hearty taste. Our Kurdish quinoa can be served as a side dish, or add tofu for a complete meal.

KURDISH QUINOA

Serves 4

3 tablespoons olive oil

½ onion, finely chopped

2 red bell peppers, finely chopped

1 cup julienned white mushrooms

2 cups julienned shiitake mushrooms

2 cups quinoa

2 cups Marinara Sauce (page 33)

4 sprigs fresh thyme

1 tablespoon salt

In a large pot, heat the olive oil over high heat. Add the onion and sauté until transparent, 1 to 2 minutes. Add the bell pepper and sauté for another minute. Add the white mushrooms and shiitake mushrooms and sauté for 1 minute. Add the quinoa and 3 cups water to the pot and reduce the heat to low. Add the Marinara Sauce, thyme, and salt and stir well. Simmer, covered, for about 40 minutes, or until the water has been absorbed. Remove sprigs of thyme before serving.

At Blossom, we like to provide healthy alternatives to traditional vegan sides, especially for those who try to balance their intake of carbohydrates. Reinventing mashed potatoes was a lot of fun with the use of sunchokes, a tasty root vegetable also known as Jerusalem artichoke. Their distinct nutty, earthy, sweet flavor makes this dish just as tasty as our classic creamy mashed potatoes.

SUNCHOKE MASH

Serves 3 as a side dish

1 pound sunchokes (about 12), peeled

2 tablespoons vegan butter

1 tablespoon finely chopped garlic

Salt and black pepper

1. Bring a medium pot of water to a boil and add the sunchokes. Boil until the sunchokes are soft, about 20 minutes. Drain the sunchokes and carefully dry them.

2. Put the sunchokes, vegan butter, and garlic in a medium bowl and whisk together until smooth. Season with salt and pepper.

Coconut milk is a texture and flavor staple for many vegan and vegetarian dishes; it truly has tremendous versatility. We were exploring ideas to expand our side dish selection, and voilà—this dish was invented! Fun fact: Former President Bill Clinton ordered this dish for delivery several times when he was in the neighborhood.

SWEET POTATO COCONUT CURRY

Serves 3 or 4

2 medium sweet potatoes, peeled and chopped into 2-inch cubes

1 teaspoon chopped garlic

4 tablespoons extra-virgin olive oil

½ medium onion, finely chopped

1 small jalapeño, chopped

½ teaspoon ground cumin

½ teaspoon ground turmeric

2 cups coconut milk

1 tablespoon sugar

1. Preheat the oven to 350°F. Lightly oil a baking sheet with a drizzle of olive oil.

2. In a medium bowl, combine the sweet potatoes, garlic, and 2 tablespoons of the olive oil and toss gently until well coated. Spread the cubes over the prepared baking sheet and bake for 20 to 30 minutes, or until soft. Remove from the oven and set aside.

3. In a medium pot, heat the remaining 2 tablespoons olive oil over medium-high heat. Add the onion and jalapeño and sauté for about 1 minute. Add the sweet potato cubes, cumin, turmeric, coconut milk, and sugar and stir well. Cook for about 5 minutes.

SOUPS

A restaurant staple, this recipe is our take on a classic soup. Lentils are a tasty and hearty member of the legume family, and a great source of protein. They're also easier to prepare than dried beans, as they cook quickly and easily with no soaking required.

LENTIL-VEGETABLE SOUP

Serves 6 to 8

2 tablespoons extra-virgin olive oil

1 tablespoon minced garlic

1 medium onion, diced

2 large ripe tomatoes, chopped

2 medium-large carrots, diced

5 celery stalks, chopped

1½ cups French lentils

2 tablespoons salt

1 tablespoon black pepper

3 bay leaves

3 sprigs fresh thyme

1 cup chopped fresh cilantro

1. In a large pot, heat the olive oil over medium-high heat. Add the garlic and sauté for 1 to 2 minutes, then add the onion and sauté for 2 to 3 minutes. Add the tomatoes and sauté for 3 to 4 minutes to cook off their liquid. Add the carrots and celery and sauté for 1 to 2 minutes. Add the lentils, salt, pepper, bay leaves, thyme, cilantro, and 9 cups water. Bring the mixture to a boil, then reduce the heat to medium and simmer until the lentils and carrots are soft, 15 to 20 minutes.

2. Serve, or continue to simmer over low heat to deepen the flavors. Make sure to remove the bay leaves before serving.

This unique and spicy soup is a favorite Blossom menu item during the winter months. It features oyster mushrooms, which add a delicately savory flavor, as well as blended zucchini, which acts as a delicious plant-based thickener.

OYSTER MUSHROOM SOUP

Serves 5 or 6

15 medium-large oyster mushrooms

2 medium zucchini: 1 coarsely chopped, 1 chopped

1 cup chopped fresh cilantro

¼ jalapeño

2 tablespoons extra-virgin olive oil

6 celery stalks, chopped

1 medium onion, chopped

1 medium-large carrot, diced

2 tablespoons salt

1. Trim off the lower inch of stem from the oyster mushrooms.

2. Combine the coarsely chopped zucchini, cilantro, jalapeño, and 8 cups water in a large bowl. Blend in 2 batches, if needed, in a high-speed blender until smooth and set aside.

3. In a large stockpot, heat the olive oil over high heat. Add the celery, onion, chopped zucchini, and carrot and sauté for 1 to 2 minutes, then reduce the heat to medium. Add the blended zucchini mixture, the salt, and the mushrooms. Increase the heat to high and bring to a boil, then reduce the heat to medium-low and simmer for 20 to 30 minutes.

4. Serve, or continue to simmer to deepen the flavors.

In this mild, creamy soup, the sweetness of the corn and coconut is well balanced by the garlic and spices. Make sure to use actual canned coconut milk and solids, rather than a coconut-based milk substitute. The coconut and corn give this soup a fantastic natural sweetness, but if you'd like, feel free to add a tablespoon of sugar.

YELLOW CORN AND COCONUT SOUP

Serves 4 or 5

2 tablespoons olive oil

½ medium onion, chopped

1 tablespoon garlic

3 cups fresh corn

Pinch of salt

Pinch of black pepper

2 bay leaves

1 sprig fresh thyme

1½ (14-ounce) cans coconut milk

1 tablespoon sugar (optional)

In a large stockpot, heat the olive oil over high heat. Add the onion and garlic and sauté for 1 to 2 minutes. Add the corn, salt, pepper, bay leaves, thyme, and 5 cups water. Bring to a boil, then reduce the heat to medium. Add the coconut milk and simmer for 15 to 20 minutes. Carefully transfer the soup to a high-speed blender, working in batches if necessary, and blend until smooth. Taste, and add the sugar (if using) and blend again.

You simply can't add too many onions to this soup! The incredibly long sautéing time makes the onions sweet and mild—just be sure to stir frequently to prevent burning.

FRENCH ONION SOUP

Serves 5 or 6

4 tablespoons extra-virgin olive oil

6 medium white or Spanish onions, chopped

1 tablespoon chopped garlic

4 bay leaves

4 sprigs fresh thyme

2 tablespoons salt

1 tablespoon black pepper

FOR THE "CHEESY" BREAD (OPTIONAL)

1 baguette, cut into 1-inch-thick slices

2 tablespoons olive oil

Pinch of salt

Pinch of black pepper

½ cup shredded vegan cheese

1. In a large pot, heat 2 tablespoons of the olive oil over high heat. Add the onions and sauté, stirring frequently, for about 3 minutes, then reduce the heat to its lowest setting and cook, stirring frequently, for 30 to 45 minutes, until the onions are deep brown and caramelized.

2. When the onions are almost finished, in a large stockpot, heat the remaining 2 tablespoons olive oil over medium heat. Add the garlic and sauté until the garlic just begins to brown. Add the onions, bay leaves, thyme, salt, pepper, and 9 cups water. Increase the heat and bring the soup to a boil. Cook for about 5 minutes, then reduce the heat to medium-low and simmer for 10 to 15 minutes. Remove the bay leaves and thyme sprigs before serving.

3. **If desired, make the "cheesy" bread:** Preheat the oven to 350°F.

4. Gently brush the baguette slices with the olive oil and sprinkle with the salt and pepper. Put the baguette slices on a baking sheet and bake for 5 minutes. Keep the oven on.

5. Ladle the soup into oven-safe bowls. Place one toasted baguette slice on top of each bowl, then top with vegan cheese. Put the bowls on a rimmed baking sheet and bake for 1 to 2 minutes, or until the cheese has melted.

Sweet potatoes are packed with nutrition, which is why they're one of Chef Francisco's favorite vegetables. They contain more beta-carotene per serving than carrots, all while tasting rich and indulgent, like you skipped your entrée and went straight for dessert. Eating good fats, like those in coconut, aids beta-carotene absorption. This soup is both tasty and a healthy powerhouse!

· SWEET POTATO AND COCONUT CREAM SOUP

Serves 4 or 5

2 tablespoons olive oil

½ medium onion, diced

1 tablespoon finely chopped garlic

3 medium sweet potatoes, peeled and cubed

2 tablespoons salt

1 tablespoon black pepper

3 cups coconut milk

½ teaspoon ground cinnamon

1 tablespoon sugar (optional)

1. In a large stockpot, heat the olive oil over high heat. Add the onion and garlic and sauté for 1 to 2 minutes. Add the sweet potatoes and sauté for 2 minutes. Add 8 cups water, the salt, and the pepper. Bring to a boil and cook until the sweet potato is soft, about 20 minutes. Add the coconut milk and cook for 5 minutes. Remove from the heat.

2. Carefully transfer the soup to a high-speed blender, working in batches if necessary, add the cinnamon and sugar (if using), and blend until smooth.

SALADS & SANDWICHES

Quinoa is one of our favorite ingredients, and for good reason. It's a complete protein, easy to cook, and tastes great hot or cold. This healthy salad features watercress—an often overlooked green, which is unfortunate, since it's so incredibly healthful! In fact, watercress has more iron than spinach, more calcium than milk, and more vitamin C than orange juice.

QUINOA SALAD

Serves 2

1½ cups dry quinoa

1 tablespoon salt, plus a pinch

1 medium red bell pepper, diced

1 cup cooked and drained black beans (canned is fine)

1 handful watercress

½ cup corn

½ cup Tahini Dressing (page 22)

1 pinch of black pepper

2 radishes, sliced

2 tablespoons toasted pumpkin seeds

¼ cup Authentic Guacamole (page 30)

1. In a medium pot, combine the quinoa, 1 tablespoon of the salt, and 3 cups water. Bring to a boil, then reduce the heat to low, cover, and simmer until the water has been absorbed, 7 to 8 minutes. Transfer to a bowl and place in the fridge to cool.

2. In a medium bowl, combine the bell pepper, black beans, watercress, corn, and tahini dressing and mix well with your hands. Add the quinoa to the bowl and mix well. Divide the salad between two plates, season with the remaining salt and the black pepper, and top with the radish, pumpkin seeds, and guacamole.

This gorgeous salad is as beautiful to look at as it is delicious to eat! The alternating red and golden beets make this dish a colorful masterpiece, and the tartness of the red wine vinegar dressing balances the natural sweetness of the beets. You can serve with any greens of your choice, but we use kale.

BEET CARPACCIO

Serves 2

1 medium-large red beet

1 medium-large golden beet

2 tablespoons extra-virgin olive oil

2 pinches of salt

2 pinches of black pepper

1 large handful kale, chopped

1 handful romaine, chopped

5 tablespoons Red Wine Vinaigrette (page 22)

3 tablespoons sliced almonds

1. Preheat the oven to 350°F.

2. Wash the beets, drizzle with the olive oil, and sprinkle with a pinch each of the salt and pepper. Wrap them individually in aluminum foil and bake for 1½ hours, or until soft. Let cool in the refrigerator for about 20 minutes. Peel and slice the beets very thinly and evenly. On each plate, layer the beets in a circle, alternating the golden and red beet layers. Place the kale and romaine in a large bowl and sprinkle with the remaining pinch each of salt and pepper. Add the vinaigrette and mix well.

3. Place a pile of the dressed greens in the middle of the beets and garnish with the almonds.

I loved Caesar salads before I became a vegan in the '90s, so I put Chef Francisco to the task of creating the perfect vegan alternative. He didn't disappoint—everyone I know who comes to Blossom comes back for more of our Caesar. In fact, we are now famous for it. We know of a guest who walks ten blocks to our Chelsea location daily, even in the cold New York City winters, just for our Caesar salad. A few years ago, our photographer, Alex, suggested putting crisp shiitake "bacon" on top, which adds a ton of that elusive umami flavor. All hail our Caesar!

CAESAR SALAD

Serves 4

1½ cups cubed bread (we prefer Italian bread or baguette)

3 tablespoons extra-virgin olive oil

Pinch of salt

Pinch of pepper

2 tablespoons capers, drained

3 heads romaine lettuce, chopped

1½ cups Caesar Dressing (page 21)

2 tablespoons Parmesan "Cheese" (page 23; optional)

1. Preheat the oven to 350°F. In a bowl, toss cubed bread with 2 tablespoons of olive oil and a pinch each of salt and pepper. Spread on a baking sheet and bake for 5 to 10 minutes, or until golden brown. Remove from the oven and allow to cool. Set aside. In a small sauté pan, heat the remaining 1 tablespoon oil over medium-high heat. Add the capers and sauté until they begin to crisp, 3 to 4 minutes. Remove from the heat and set aside.

2. Put the romaine in a large bowl. Add the Caesar dressing and mix well.

3. Divide the salad among four plates, then garnish with toasted capers, croutons, and vegan Parmesan, if desired.

Everyone wants the health benefits of eating raw kale, but it's quite a fibrous and tough green! The great thing about our kale salad is that the beneficial fats in the avocado and the acidity of the citrus in the Almond-Ginger Dressing break down the kale and make it softer and easier to eat. Now you can have your kale and eat it, too!

RAW KALE SALAD

Serves 2

3 handfuls kale, chopped

3 tablespoons chopped scallion

¼ cup diced red bell pepper

6 tablespoons Almond-Ginger Dressing (page 21)

1 ripe avocado, halved and pitted

2 pinches of salt

Pinch of black pepper

Put the kale in a large bowl. Add the scallion, bell pepper, Almond-Ginger Dressing, and avocado and mash the salad with your hands to mix and distribute the avocado. Massage the kale until it begins to soften. Add the salt and black pepper and serve.

This salad was first served more than one hundred years ago at the famous Waldorf-Astoria hotel here in New York City. Today, it feels like a relic of another time, but we think it's worth bringing back! The tartness of the Granny Smith apples and the lime juice in the dressing make for a perfectly refreshing summer salad.

WALDORF SALAD

Serves 2 or 3

FOR THE DRESSING

¾ cup vegan mayonnaise, store-bought or homemade (page 27)

Juice of 1 lime

Pinch of salt

Pinch of black pepper

FOR THE SALAD

1 head romaine, chopped

¾ cup chopped celery (about 3 stalks)

2 cups diced Granny Smith apples (1 or 2 apples)

½ cup walnuts

¼ cup raisins

1. Make the dressing: In a medium bowl, whisk together the vegan mayonnaise, lime juice, salt, and pepper until well combined.

2. Make the salad: In a large bowl, combine the romaine, celery, apples, walnuts, and raisins and mix well. Add the dressing and mix again to combine. Serve in small bowls.

When you cook with vegetables as the star ingredients, it's always important to start with the freshest quality organic produce you can find. Think of this sandwich as your "farmers' market sandwich"—it's best right after a trip to your local market. You might want to make some extra eggplant spread; you're going to want to eat it on crackers after you're done with the sandwich!

ROASTED VEGETABLE SANDWICH

Serves 3

2 red bell peppers

1 medium eggplant, halved lengthwise

3 tablespoons extra-virgin olive oil

2 teaspoons salt, plus more as needed

½ teaspoon black pepper, plus more as needed

6 tablespoons vegan mayonnaise, store-bought or homemade (page 27)

1 green zucchini

1 yellow squash

1 teaspoon chopped garlic

2 handfuls spinach

6 slices bread

1. Preheat the oven to 350°F.

2. Put the bell peppers on a baking sheet and roast until the skins begin to peel off. (Alternatively, blacken the peppers directly over a gas burner on the stovetop.) Place the blackened peppers in a heat-safe bowl, cover with plastic wrap, and set aside for 10 minutes to loosen the skins. Keep the oven on.

3. Drizzle the eggplant halves with 1 tablespoon of the olive oil and season with a pinch each of salt and black pepper. Put the eggplant on a baking sheet and roast for 15 to 20 minutes, or until very soft. Remove the eggplant from the oven when soft (keep the oven on) and scoop the flesh into a food processor or blender with a spoon. Add the vegan mayonnaise, 2 teaspoons salt, and ½ teaspoon black pepper. Process until smooth, then set aside.

4. Oil a baking sheet with a drizzle of olive oil. Thinly slice the zucchini and squash lengthwise (a mandoline slicer does a good job of this). Lay the strips of zucchini and

RECIPE CONTINUES

squash flat on the prepared baking sheet. Drizzle with 1 tablespoon of the olive oil and season with a pinch each of salt and pepper. Roast for 5 to 10 minutes, then remove and set aside.

5. Remove the peppers from the bowl. Using a rag, rub the peppers—the blackened skin should come off quite easily. Slice open the peppers and remove the seeds, ribs, and stem of one pepper. Julienne the roasted pepper slices.

6. In a large skillet, heat the remaining 1 tablespoon olive oil over medium-high heat. Add the garlic and sauté for 1 to 2 minutes. Add the spinach and sauté for 1 to 2 minutes.

7. To assemble each sandwich, coat one side of each slice of bread with the eggplant spread, top with a zucchini slice, a squash slice, strips of roasted bell pepper, and spinach, and finish with another slice of bread. Enjoy!

A Blossom original, this flavorful sandwich has been on our menu since the beginning. It's a classic take on the BLT, with the addition of crispy fried tofu, which takes it to a new level of heartiness. The aioli adds fantastic spice. We use tempeh bacon in our sandwich, but you can also enjoy it with a vegan bacon of your choice.

TOFU BLT

Serves 3

1 (14-ounce) block firm or extra-firm tofu, drained

1 tablespoon tamari

1 cup soy milk

½ cup all-purpose flour

1 cup panko bread crumbs

2 cups grapeseed, safflower, or sunflower oil

6 slices multigrain bread, toasted

3 tablespoons Chipotle Aioli (page 29)

3 large lettuce leaves

1 large tomato, sliced

9 slices vegan bacon, cooked

1. Turn the tofu block onto its skinny side and slice it lengthwise into three even slices. Put the tofu slices in a deep container and add 4 cups water and the tamari. Cover and marinate in the refrigerator for at least 8 hours.

2. In a medium bowl, whisk together the soy milk and flour. Put the panko in another medium bowl. Drain the tofu slices, then dredge them in the soy milk mixture. Dredge them again in the panko, taking care to fully coat each slice. Set the breaded tofu slices on a rack and let sit for 10 minutes for the breading to dry.

3. In a deep skillet, heat the oil over medium-high heat to 350°F. Carefully submerge the tofu slices in the oil (do not overcrowd the pan) and pan-fry until they begin to brown. Remove from the oil and drain on a paper towel.

4. To assemble each sandwich, spread the Chipotle Aioli on the bread and add a lettuce leaf, tomato slice, 3 slices of the vegan bacon, and a slice of breaded tofu. Top with another slice of bread and carefully slice it in half on an angle.

NOTE: The tofu must be marinated for at least 8 hours, so plan ahead.

We took traditional grilled cheese to the next level with tempeh bacon, sliced tomato, and onion. People love this so much that we actually started to cut the sandwich into quarters and serve it as party appetizers! Perfect when served with a tomato soup for a classic American lunch combo.

GRILLED CHEESE

Serves 1

1 tablespoon vegan mayonnaise, store-bought or homemade (page 27)

2 slices multigrain bread

2 slices fresh tomato

1 thin slice red onion

⅓ cup shredded vegan cheese

3 slices vegan bacon, cooked

1½ teaspoons vegan butter

1. Spread the vegan mayonnaise on one side of each slice of bread. Top with the tomato, onion, vegan cheese, and vegan bacon.

2. In a small sauté pan, melt the vegan butter over medium heat. Place the sandwich in the pan and cover, flipping periodically to brown evenly on both sides and melt the cheese.

A classic Blossom sandwich—we couldn't take this off our menu if we tried! Crispy Cajun-spiced seitan with avocado and our signature Chipotle Aioli . . . what's not to love? We serve ours on rosemary focaccia, but you can use the bread of your choice. You can also add caramelized onions or enjoy this wonderful spiced seitan without the bread—trust us, it's that good.

SOUTHERN SEITAN SANDWICH

Serves 4

½ cup adobo seasoning

½ cup Cajun seasoning

2 cups bread crumbs

1 cup all-purpose flour

1 cup soy milk

1 tablespoon black pepper

1 pound seitan, sliced ½ inch thick

2 tablespoons olive oil

2 medium onions, sliced

2 cups grapeseed, safflower, or sunflower oil

8 slices focaccia bread (or bread of your choice), toasted

½ cup Chipotle Aioli (page 29)

2 fresh avocados, halved, pitted, and sliced

1 head lettuce or other greens

1. In a large bowl, combine the adobo seasoning, Cajun seasoning, and bread crumbs. In a second large bowl, combine the flour, soy milk, and pepper. Dredge the seitan slices in the soy milk mixture, then dredge them in the seasoned bread crumbs, taking care to fully coat the slices. Set aside.

2. In a large skillet, heat the olive oil over low heat. Add the onions and sauté for 30 minutes to caramelize them. Remove from the heat and set aside.

3. In a deep-sided pan, heat the oil to 350°F. Add the breaded seitan slices (be careful not to crowd the pan) and pan-fry until golden brown and crispy. Remove the slices from the oil and place them on paper towels to drain excess oil.

4. To assemble each sandwich, spread the Chipotle Aioli on a slice of bread and add a slice of the breaded seitan, avocado slices, caramelized onions, and lettuce. Top with a second slice of bread and enjoy!

BRUNCH

When we created our brunch menu, we knew that pancakes were a must. Rather than going with the traditional white or whole wheat flour, we thought it would be great to maintain the irresistible taste of a pancake but replace the flour with a rich protein to start the day. The protein powerhouse—quinoa—works perfectly in this recipe. Most people think it's a grain, but it's actually a seed! These pancakes are a mouthwatering meal that will satisfy *and* energize! Serve them with a great maple syrup, cut strawberries, and our Coconut Cream on the side. Bon appétit!

FLUFFY QUINOA PANCAKES

Serves 4; makes 12 pancakes

2 cups quinoa flour

½ cup packed light brown sugar

4 teaspoons baking powder

1 tablespoon ground cinnamon

2½ cups soy milk

2 tablespoons extra-virgin olive oil

1 tablespoon vanilla extract

2 tablespoons vegan butter

1 cup mixed berries

½ cup Grade A maple syrup

½ cup Coconut Cream (page 26)

1. In a large bowl, whisk together the quinoa flour, brown sugar, baking powder, and cinnamon until well combined. In a separate medium bowl, whisk together the soy milk, oil, and vanilla until well combined. Whisk the wet ingredients into the dry ingredients until well combined. Let sit for 5 minutes.

2. On a griddle or in a skillet, melt the butter over medium heat. Add the pancake batter in ¼-cup scoops and cook until small bubbles begin to form on the pancake's surface, then flip and cook on the second side for approximately 1 to 2 minutes.

3. Serve three pancakes per person, and top with fresh berries, maple syrup, and Coconut Cream!

Our French toast is addictive! You will quickly see that there's no need for eggs. So simple to make, yet with all the sweet goodness and flavor of a great authentic French toast. Try it with our Tofu Scramble (page 128) for a great combination of sweet and savory. I suggest using baguette slices and preparing it well done for the absolute best result. It's a perfect brunch delight or a guilt-free snack, and it's extra delicious when topped with cinnamon, berries, and even Coconut Cream on the side. A true toast to savor!

FRENCH TOAST

Serves 4

1½ cups all-purpose flour

2 cups soy milk

1 tablespoon ground cinnamon

1 cup maple syrup

1½ teaspoons vanilla extract

24 slices baguette (about
  1 inch thick)

2 tablespoons vegan butter

½ cup blueberries

½ cup sliced strawberries

½ cup sliced banana

Coconut Cream (page 26)

1. Preheat the oven to 350°F. Oil a baking sheet with a drizzle of olive oil.

2. In a large bowl, whisk together the flour, soy milk, cinnamon, ½ cup of the maple syrup, and the vanilla until well combined. Slice the baguette slices in half, into triangles. Dredge the baguette slices in the flour and soy milk batter, making sure each slice is well coated.

3. In a large skillet, melt 1 tablespoon of the vegan butter over medium-high heat. Place the coated bread triangles in the skillet and cook for 2 minutes on each side, or until they begin to crisp. Remove from the pan, and place on the prepared baking sheet. Bake for 5 to 10 minutes for extra crispiness!

4. Remove from the oven and serve with fresh fruit, Coconut Cream, and the remaining maple syrup!

One of my favorites to make on a weekend morning. Every time I host nonvegan guests and tell them I'm making this dish, I can see the skepticism in their eyes . . . yet without fail, not only do they clean their plates, but they ask me for the recipe! Very important tip, though—be sure to drain the water out of the tofu before you crumble it for a light and fluffy scramble. Follow the recipe, but also feel free to improvise with wild mushrooms, bell peppers, scallions, and fresh avocado on the side. Scramble your way, be as creative as you like, and enjoy!

TOFU SCRAMBLE

Serves 4

1 (14-ounce) block firm or extra-firm tofu, drained

1½ teaspoons ground turmeric

1½ teaspoons salt

¼ teaspoon black pepper

1 tablespoon vegan butter

⅓ cup chopped onion

½ cup chopped mushrooms

1 cup chopped tomatoes

1 cup spinach

1. Using your hands, crumble the tofu into a large bowl. Add the turmeric, salt, and pepper, and mix well. Set aside.

2. In a large skillet, melt the vegan butter over high heat. Add the onion and sauté for 1 minute. Add the mushrooms and sauté for another minute. Add the tomatoes and the tofu mixture and sauté for 2 minutes. Add the spinach and sauté until wilted. Serve.

Simple to make, but absolutely exploding with flavor, this breakfast burrito is filled with our famous tofu scramble and vegan sausage. Feel free to add your favorite hot sauce to the mix if you're craving some spice, or a ripe avocado for a traditional Mexican flavor combination.

BREAKFAST BURRITO

Serves 4

2 (14-ounce) blocks firm or extra-firm tofu, drained

1 tablespoon ground turmeric

3 tablespoons chopped scallions

¼ cup chopped red bell pepper

½ cup cooked black beans (canned is fine)

½ cup cooked brown rice

1 tablespoon vegan butter

1½ cups chopped vegan sausage

1½ teaspoons salt

¼ teaspoon black pepper

4 large tortillas

2 ripe avocados, halved, pitted, and sliced

Chipotle Tomatillo Salsa (page 30; optional)

Sour Cream (page 27; optional)

1. Using your hands, crumble the tofu into a large bowl. Add the turmeric, scallions, bell pepper, black beans, and brown rice. Mix well. Set aside.

2. In a large skillet, melt the vegan butter over medium-high heat. Add the vegan sausage and sauté until it begins to brown, 1 to 2 minutes. Add the tofu and vegetable mixture and sauté for 2 to 3 minutes. Add the salt and black pepper and stir.

3. Set one tortilla on each of four plates. Divide the filling evenly among the tortillas. Add ½ sliced avocado to each tortilla and roll up tightly into a burrito. Garnish with the salsa and Sour Cream, if desired.

I tasted eggs Florentine for the first time late in life, and was so amazed at the flavors. When we decided to offer a brunch menu, Chef Francisco was able to create a phenomenal tofu Florentine. It has the same protein punch as the original, with sulfuric notes from the sautéed spinach that truly reminds you of the flavor of eggs. A great all-year-round dish, it's perfect for breakfast or for a weekend brunch.

TOFU FLORENTINE

Serves 4

2 (14-ounce) blocks firm or extra-firm tofu

3 tablespoons tamari

Leaves from 2 sprigs fresh rosemary

Leaves from 6 sprigs fresh thyme

4 tablespoons extra-virgin olive oil

1 bunch spinach

Salt and black pepper

4 English muffins, split and toasted

8 tablespoons Hollandaise Sauce (page 29)

NOTE: Marinating the tofu for at least a few hours is key to this dish, so plan ahead.

1. Using a 3- to 4-inch round cookie cutter, slice through the top of the tofu block. Slice the resulting cylinder crosswise into four equal pieces to create four circles of tofu. Repeat with the other tofu block. Put the tofu slices in a deep container and add the tamari, rosemary, thyme, and 6 cups water. Marinate for 3 to 5 hours or up to overnight for an even deeper flavor.

2. In a skillet, heat 2 tablespoons of the olive oil over medium heat. Add the tofu slices and sauté for 1 to 2 minutes. Remove the tofu and set aside.

3. In the same pan, heat the remaining 2 tablespoons olive oil over medium-high heat. Add the spinach and salt and pepper and sauté for 1 to 2 minutes, just until the spinach is fully wilted. Remove from the heat.

4. To serve, plate two toasted English muffin halves, cut-sides up, on each of four plates. Top evenly with the spinach, followed by the tofu, and finally drizzling 1 tablespoon Hollandaise Sauce over each English muffin half.

ENTRÉES

I am especially proud of this dish because it is so inventive: a vegetable-based spin on a traditional risotto. We replaced the rice with cauliflower, which is an incredibly versatile vegetable. To add a meaty kick, we added shiitakes to this dish to balance the milder taste of the cauliflower. It's incredible how many other restaurants and chefs are now using cauliflower as a meat or grain replacement!

CAULIFLOWER RISOTTO

Serves 2

5 tablespoons vegan butter

1 tablespoon minced garlic, plus 1 garlic clove

1½ teaspoons salt, plus more as needed

½ teaspoon black pepper, plus more as needed

1¼ cups polenta

1 medium head cauliflower

2 whole, peeled shallots plus 2 tablespoons chopped shallots

5 tablespoons olive oil

½ cup white wine

3 tablespoons chopped fresh parsley

2 cups sliced shiitake mushrooms

1. In a large pot, combine 1 tablespoon of the vegan butter, the minced garlic, 1 teaspoon of the salt, ½ teaspoon of the pepper, and 3 cups water. Bring to a boil. Add the polenta and stir until the water has been absorbed, 1 to 2 minutes. Remove from the pan and spread to a ½-inch thickness on a lightly oiled baking sheet.

2. Remove the tough stem of the cauliflower and discard. Coarsely chop the head of the cauliflower and place in a food processor. Pulse seven or eight times, or until it is finely minced, similar to the size and consistency of grains of rice. Divide the cauliflower into two equal portions.

3. Fill a large pot with water and add half the cauliflower, the whole shallots, and the garlic clove. Bring to a boil, and boil for 20 to 25 minutes, or until the cauliflower is soft. Drain the water and transfer the boiled cauliflower, shallots, and garlic to a high-speed blender. Blend until smooth.

4. Remove the polenta from the refrigerator and use a large thin-rimmed glass or a cookie cutter to cut it into rounds. Set aside.

RECIPE CONTINUES

5. In a large skillet, heat 2 tablespoons of the olive oil over medium-high heat. Add the chopped shallot and sauté for 1 to 2 minutes, then add the rest of the minced cauliflower and stir well. Add the white wine and sauté for 1 to 2 minutes, then add the pureed cauliflower and stir. Add 1 cup water, ½ teaspoon salt, and 2 tablespoons of the vegan butter and stir. Add the parsley and stir to combine. The resulting mixture should be a risotto-like consistency.

6. In a medium skillet, heat 2 tablespoons of the olive oil over medium-high heat. Add the mushrooms and a pinch each of salt and pepper. Sauté until the mushrooms begin to brown. Set aside.

7. In a separate medium sauté pan, heat the remaining 1 tablespoon of olive oil over medium heat. Add the polenta cakes and sauté for 1 to 2 minutes on each side, or until golden brown on both sides.

8. To assemble, divide the polenta cakes between two plates, then top with the cauliflower risotto and finally the sautéed mushrooms.

This dish is truly one of my favorites, and while it is relatively easy to make, it is by no means a simple dish. The combination of the miso, white wine, and our signature Cashew Cream makes for a velvety, "buttery"-rich flavor. This risotto is my lunch and/or dinner party go-to. I make it very frequently for friends and am always asked for the recipe. So here you go! It's just as great on a cold winter night as it is with a glass of white wine on a spring or summer evening. Guard any leftovers you have—they are just as delicious reheated for lunch the next day! This dish has all the right taste sensations—savory, salty, sweet, but mostly sumptuous!

MUSHROOM MISO MUSTARD RISOTTO

Serves 2

½ cup olive oil

½ medium onion, finely chopped

1½ cups Arborio rice

1⅓ cups white wine

1 cup shiitake mushrooms, stemmed and sliced

1 cup cremini mushrooms, cut into ½-inch pieces

1 cup king trumpet mushrooms, sliced into ¼-inch medallions

1½ teaspoons salt, plus more as needed

¼ teaspoon black pepper, plus more as needed

1. In a large pot, heat 2 tablespoons of the olive oil over medium-high heat. Add the onion and sauté for 2 to 3 minutes, or until translucent. Add the rice, stir for 1 minute, then add 1 cup of the white wine and 3 cups water. Bring to a boil, then reduce the heat to medium and cover. Simmer, covered, for 10 to 12 minutes, or until most of the water has been absorbed and the rice is al dente.

2. In a large skillet, heat 2 tablespoons of the olive oil over medium heat. Add the shiitakes, creminis, trumpet mushrooms, and a pinch each of salt and pepper. Sauté until the mushrooms begin to brown.

3. In a large skillet, heat 2 tablespoons of the olive oil over medium heat. Add the shallots and sauté for 1 to 2 minutes.

RECIPE CONTINUES

1 tablespoon chopped shallot

1½ cups Cashew Cream
  (page 26)

1 cup vegetable stock

2 tablespoons white miso

1 tablespoon Dijon mustard

1½ teaspoons tamari

Add the risotto, mushroom blend, remaining ⅓ cup white wine, the Cashew Cream, stock, salt, and pepper. Sauté until most of the liquid has evaporated.

4. While the liquid evaporates from the risotto, in a small bowl, whisk together the miso, mustard, and tamari until smooth. Add to the risotto and cook for about 8 minutes, or until the rice is soft. Serve.

This dish was born for the "in bloom" menu that we introduced in 2015, in which we create dishes made from vegetables of the season. We enjoy working to create dishes that showcase the natural flavors of vegetables without compromising on taste. This was one of the first ideas Chef Francisco and I had: a risotto using shredded zucchini and Broccolini instead of rice. The white wine sauce adds amazing flavor, and the dish proves that vegetables can truly stand on their own as the stars of a meal! This is fantastic to enjoy in the spring and summer.

ZUCCHINI RISOTTO

Serves 4

4 medium zucchini

12 tricolor baby carrots

4 baby fennel bulbs, halved

2 cups fresh or frozen green peas

Zest of 1 lime

4 tablespoons olive oil

1½ teaspoons finely chopped garlic

2 tablespoons chopped shallot

2 cups finely minced Broccolini

⅓ cup white wine

2 tablespoons vegan butter

1 tablespoon salt

1½ teaspoons black pepper

2 tablespoons fresh lemon juice

1. Slice the ends off the zucchini, then slice in half lengthwise. Using a spoon, scoop out the middle of the zucchini that contains the seeds and discard. (This part of the vegetable contains too much water.)

2. Bring two medium pots of water to a boil. Fill two small bowls with ice and water. Add the baby carrots and baby fennel to one pot and boil for 5 to 10 minutes. When the baby carrots and fennel are soft, transfer them to one bowl of ice water to halt the cooking process.

3. Add the peas to the other pot of boiling water and boil for 2 to 3 minutes if fresh, 3 to 4 minutes if frozen. Transfer the peas to the second bowl of ice water to halt the cooking process. Drain the peas and put them in a high-speed blender. Add the lime zest and blend until smooth, while slowly adding ½ cup water. Set aside. Add the zucchini to a food processor, and pulse until it becomes ricelike in consistency. Using cheesecloth or a thin kitchen towel,

RECIPE CONTINUES

squeeze out as much moisture from the zucchini as possible. This will lead to a firmer texture. Set aside.

4. In a large skillet, heat 2 to 3 tablespoons of the olive oil over medium-high heat. Add the garlic. Add the carrots and fennel, cover, and cook, stirring occasionally, until the vegetables are just beginning to caramelize.

5. In a separate skillet, heat the remaining 1 tablespoon olive oil over medium heat. Add the shallots and sauté for about 1 minute, or until they just begin to brown. Add the zucchini and Broccolini and sauté for 1 to 2 minutes, or until the vegetables begin to soften. Add the white wine, vegan butter, salt, pepper, blended green peas, and lemon juice and sauté for 2 to 3 minutes, taking care not to overcook (or the zucchini will become soggy).

6. To serve, divide the zucchini and Broccolini mixture among four bowls and spoon the carrots and fennel on top.

Healthy, hearty, sweet . . . without the guilt! Most gnocchi tends to be rich in taste but also in calories. We created our own light, vegetable-based gnocchi using gluten-free flour and butternut squash. Served with our rich cashew cream, as well as beets and spinach, this dish is a sensory feast of sweet and savory. This gnocchi works well as an appetizer, too.

BUTTERNUT SQUASH GNOCCHI

Serves 3 or 4

2 butternut squashes, peeled, halved, and seeded

1 large red beet, peeled, halved

4 tablespoons olive oil

2 pinches of salt

2 pinches of black pepper

3 cups all-purpose flour (substitute rice flour for gluten-free), plus more as needed

5 tablespoons agave nectar

2 tablespoons chopped shallot

1 tablespoon chopped fresh basil

⅓ cup white wine

4 cups Cashew Cream (page 26)

2 handfuls fresh spinach

Cherry tomatoes (optional)

1. Preheat the oven to 350°F.

2. Lightly coat the squash and the beet with 2 tablespoons of the olive oil and sprinkle with a pinch each of salt and pepper. Wrap with aluminum foil and roast until soft, about 30 minutes. Remove from the oven and carefully unwrap. Allow the beet to cool, and then cut it into cubes. Set aside.

3. In a large bowl or dish, mash the butternut squash. Wrap the mashed squash in a double layer of cheesecloth and twist the ends of the cheesecloth until liquid begins to drip from the squash. Continue to gently squeeze and twist until all the liquid has been removed. Transfer the squash to a large bowl and discard the cheesecloth.

4. Add the flour and agave to the bowl with the squash and mix it well using your hands. (Feel free to add small amounts of additional flour if dough is too moist.) On a well-floured work surface, roll small handfuls of the dough with your hands into ½-inch-thick ropes. Cut the ropes crosswise into 1½-inch-long gnocchi.

RECIPE CONTINUES

5. Bring a large pot of water to a boil. Fill a large bowl with ice and water. Boil the gnocchi for 4 to 5 minutes, or until they begin to float. Remove the gnocchi from the boiling water and transfer to the ice water to halt the cooking process.

6. In a large sauté pan, heat the remaining 2 tablespoons olive oil over medium heat. Add the shallot and basil. Sauté for 1 to 2 minutes. Add the white wine (be careful—it may flame). Add the Cashew Cream and a pinch each of salt and pepper. Add the gnocchi and sauté until the sauce begins to thicken. Add the spinach and stir gently until wilted. Top with the cubed beet, and serve garnished with quartered cherry tomatoes, if desired.

Another one of our most popular dishes, and incredibly easy to make at home. You can pull it together very quickly, and it tastes great with regular or gluten-free pasta. It's so rich and creamy that your nonvegan friends will be shocked to learn there's no actual cheese or butter in the dish!

FETTUCCINE WITH ALFREDO CASHEW CREAM

Serves 4

2 tablespoons olive oil

1 tablespoon chopped shallot

2 cups sliced shiitake mushrooms

⅓ cup white wine

4 cups Cashew Cream (page 26)

¼ cup Parmesan "Cheese" (page 23), plus more for serving

1 (16-ounce) package pasta of your choice (we use fettucine), prepared

2 handfuls fresh spinach

1½ teaspoons salt

1 teaspoon black pepper

4 cherry tomatoes, for garnish (optional)

In a large skillet, heat the olive oil over high heat. Add the shallot and sauté for 1 to 2 minutes. Add the mushrooms, white wine, Cashew Cream, and Parmesan "Cheese." Stir well and cook for 4 to 5 minutes. Add the cooked pasta, and toss gently. Add the spinach, salt, and pepper, and gently fold in the spinach until wilted. Serve, garnished with cherry tomato and additional Parmesan, if desired.

Bellissimo Bolognese! You can make this hearty seitan-based sauce with any pasta of your liking—we prefer a classic spaghetti. The finely minced seitan stands in for the traditionally served beef or pork, without compromising on flavor or texture. Add some garlic bread, and you've got yourself a traditional Italian dinner!

PASTA BOLOGNESE

Serves 3 or 4

8 celery stalks, coarsely chopped

1 medium-large carrot, coarsely chopped

½ to 1 pound seitan, chopped

2 tablespoons extra-virgin olive oil

½ medium onion, finely chopped

1 tablespoon minced garlic

4 bay leaves

5 cups Marinara Sauce (page 33)

2 cups soy milk

1½ tablespoons salt

1½ teaspoons black pepper

1 (16-ounce) package spaghetti, cooked, for serving

Parmesan "Cheese," for serving (page 23; optional)

1. Put the celery and carrot in a food processor and process until finely minced; transfer to a bowl. Put the seitan in the food processor and process for about 15 seconds, until finely chopped; add to the bowl with the celery and carrot and set aside.

2. In a large pot, heat the olive oil over high heat. Add the onion and garlic and sauté until the onion is translucent. Add the seitan, celery, and carrot and sauté for 1 to 2 minutes. Add the bay leaves and the Marinara Sauce and reduce the heat to low. Add the soy milk, salt, pepper, and 1 cup water and simmer for about 10 minutes.

3. Serve the sauce over the pasta. Finish with Parmesan "Cheese," if desired.

Done the right way, cooking is an art . . . and Chef Francisco is our artist extraordinaire! The way he creatively experiments with ingredients to invent different flavors and works magic with spices never fails to amaze me. Here is one of his unique, signature dishes. You can make this dish year round, but in my mind it's ideal to enjoy in the fall and winter. The sophisticated combination of the sweet potato, curry, coconut, and horseradish flavors will come together in a masterpiece in your kitchen!

CURRIED STUFFED SWEET POTATO

Serves 2

1 large sweet potato, peeled and halved

1 tablespoon extra-virgin olive oil

1 tablespoon salt, plus a pinch

Pinch of black pepper

1 cup lentils

FOR THE HORSERADISH CRÈME

⅓ cup Vegan Mayonnaise (page 27)

⅓ cup minced fresh horseradish

1 teaspoon fresh lemon juice

Pinch of salt

Pinch of black pepper

FOR THE CURRY SAUCE

1 (14-ounce) can coconut milk

1 cup natural peanut butter

1. Preheat the oven to 350°F. Oil a baking sheet.

2. Drizzle the sweet potato with 1 tablespoon olive oil and a pinch each of salt and pepper. Place on the prepared baking sheet and bake for 45 minutes, or until soft.

3. While the sweet potato is baking, place the lentils in a large pot, add 8 cups water and remaining 1 tablespoon salt, and bring to a boil over high heat. Cover, reduce the heat to medium, and cook until the lentils are soft, 15 to 20 minutes. Drain and set aside.

4. **Make the horseradish crème:** In a small bowl, whisk together the Vegan Mayonnaise, horseradish, lemon juice, salt, and pepper until smooth. Set aside.

5. **Make the curry sauce:** In a medium pot, combine the coconut milk, peanut butter, garlic powder, curry powder, salt, and 1 cup water and whisk until smooth. Bring to a boil,

RECIPE CONTINUES

1 tablespoon garlic powder

1 tablespoon curry powder

1½ teaspoons salt

2 tablespoons chopped scallion

6 tablespoons olive oil

1 tablespoon minced garlic

1 medium baby eggplant, diced

½ medium onion, finely
chopped

½ cup chopped walnuts

1 teaspoon paprika

1 teaspoon chili powder

1 teaspoon ground cumin

1 teaspoon dried oregano

3 cups vegetable stock

1½ teaspoons salt

Pinch of black pepper

2 bunches collard greens

then reduce the heat to low. Cook for 1 minute, then add the scallion. Remove from the heat, cover, and set aside.

6. In a large skillet, heat 2 tablespoons of the olive oil over high heat. Add ½ tablespoon of the garlic and sauté for 1 minute, then add the eggplant and reduce the heat to medium-low. Sauté until the eggplant is browned on all sides. Set aside.

7. In a separate skillet, heat 2 tablespoons of the olive oil over high heat. Add the onion and sauté for 2 to 3 minutes, or until translucent. Add the drained lentils, walnuts, paprika, chili powder, cumin, oregano, and stock. Reduce the heat to medium and add the salt and pepper. Cook until the water has almost evaporated, about 10 minutes. Add the cooked eggplant and cook, stirring frequently, for 2 minutes more.

8. In a separate skillet, heat the remaining 2 tablespoons olive oil over high heat. Add the remaining ½ tablespoon garlic and sauté for 1 minute. Add the collard greens and sauté for 1 to 2 minutes, or until wilted and soft.

9. To assemble, scoop a spoonful of the flesh from the center of each sweet potato with a spoon to create room for the filling. Pour ½ cup of sauce on the bottom of each plate, followed by the collard greens, sweet potato, and lentil-walnut filling. Drizzle with the horseradish crème.

A tower of flavor! Chickpeas are so versatile that they can be a base for so many wonderful dishes. They also happen to be one of my favorite legumes. An "in bloom" favorite, the chickpea cake in this dish could be its own entrée, but paired with fantastic layers of vegetables, it really comes to life!

AUTUMN TOWER

Serves 4

FOR THE TEMPEH

2 (8-ounce) packages tempeh

¼ cup sugar

2½ tablespoons Dijon mustard

1 tablespoon chili powder

1½ teaspoons paprika

4 garlic cloves

1½ tablespoons finely chopped shallots

5 tablespoons fresh lemon juice

FOR THE TOMATO SAUCE

6 yellow tomatoes, quartered

1 tablespoon chopped fresh garlic

2 tablespoons chopped fresh basil

2 tablespoons olive oil

1 tablespoon salt

1 teaspoon black pepper

1 tablespoon sugar

1. Make the tempeh: Slice the tempeh in half widthwise, then thinly slice each piece to create 4 evenly sized slices (you should have 8 slices total). Use a 2-inch-diameter cookie cutter to cut the slices into medallions. (If you don't have a cookie cutter, simply slice them into 2-inch squares.)

2. Bring a medium pot of water to a rolling boil and add the tempeh medallions. Boil for 10 minutes, then drain and set aside.

3. In a blender, combine the sugar, mustard, chili powder, paprika, garlic, shallots, lemon juice, and 4 cups water and blend until smooth. Pour the marinade into a medium bowl or pan, add the tempeh medallions, cover, and marinate in the refrigerator for at least 8 hours or up to overnight.

4. Make the tomato sauce: Put the tomatoes in a high-speed blender and add 4 cups water. Blend until smooth. Pour the blended tomatoes into a large skillet and add the garlic, basil, olive oil, salt, pepper, and sugar. Bring to a boil over high heat, then reduce the heat to maintain a simmer and cook for 10 to 15 minutes. Set aside.

RECIPE CONTINUES

FOR THE ROASTED VEGETABLES

6 small Yukon Gold potatoes, chopped into 1-inch cubes

Leaves from 2 sprigs fresh rosemary

4 tablespoons olive oil

1 teaspoon salt, plus a pinch

½ teaspoon black pepper, plus a pinch

1 tablespoon finely chopped garlic

2 medium beets

FOR THE CHICKPEA CAKES

3 cups drained canned chickpeas

½ medium onion, chopped

½ cup fresh cilantro, chopped

1 teaspoon salt

½ teaspoon black pepper

2 tablespoons olive oil

5. Make the roasted vegetables: Preheat the oven to 350°F.

6. Put the potatoes in a large bowl. Add the rosemary, 2 tablespoons of the olive oil, salt, pepper, and garlic. Toss gently and spread the mixture on a baking sheet. Roast for 25 to 35 minutes, or until soft.

7. Sprinkle the whole beets with 2 tablespoons olive oil and a pinch each of salt and pepper, wrap in aluminum foil, and roast along with the potatoes for 10 to 15 minutes, or until soft. Remove from the oven and allow to cool. Slice into ¼-inch-wide slices, set aside.

8. Make the chickpea cakes: Put the chickpeas in a food processor and process until well pureed. Transfer the pureed chickpeas to a large bowl and mix with the onion, cilantro, salt, and pepper.

9. In a large sauté pan, heat the olive oil over medium heat. Add the chickpea mixture and sauté, stirring frequently, until golden brown, 5 to 10 minutes. Use a 3½-inch-diameter cookie cutter to create small chickpea cakes by filling the cutter with 1 inch of the sautéed chickpea mixture. (You can also form the cakes by hand once the mixture has cooled slightly.) You should be able to make four cakes.

10. Make the asparagus and potatoes: Bring a medium pot of water to a boil. Add the asparagus and cook for 30 to 60 seconds. Drain.

11. In a medium bowl, stir together the vegan mayonnaise, parsley, garlic, salt, and pepper. Add the roasted potatoes and the asparagus and toss gently until well coated. Set aside.

FOR THE ASPARAGUS AND POTATOES

5 stalks asparagus, chopped into 1-inch pieces

3 tablespoons vegan mayonnaise, store-bought or homemade (page 27)

1 tablespoon chopped fresh parsley

1½ teaspoons chopped garlic

Pinch of salt

Pinch of black pepper

2 tablespoons olive oil

12. In a large sauté pan, heat the olive oil over medium heat. Add the marinated tempeh medallions and sauté, flipping frequently, until well heated through.

13. To serve, divide the sauce among four plates and top with a chickpea cake. Add a layer of the potato and asparagus mixture, followed by the marinated tempeh. Garnish with sliced roasted beets. Enjoy!

NOTE: This dish takes a little longer to prepare and the tempeh should marinate for at least 8 hours, but it will be worth the time you've invested.

This is one of our most beloved dishes at Blossom. The natural roasted sweetness of the root vegetables is balanced perfectly by the tangy truffle cream sauce. The crusted tofu and gently toasted pistachios finish the dish with great looks and taste. You can make this dish year round, but the flavors come alive most in spring and summer. Pairs perfectly with a glass of white wine.

PISTACHIO-CRUSTED TOFU

Serves 2

1 (14-ounce) block firm or extra-firm tofu, drained

¼ cup tamari or soy sauce

1 sweet potato, chopped into 1-inch cubes

1 rutabaga, chopped into 1-inch cubes

2 tablespoons olive oil

2 teaspoons salt

2 cups raw unsalted pistachios

½ teaspoon black pepper, plus 2 pinches

1 cup vegan mayonnaise, store-bought or homemade (page 27)

3 tablespoons truffle oil

2 tablespoons fresh lemon juice

1. Slice the tofu into three even slices, then cut each slice in half to form six triangles. Put the tamari, tofu slices, and 3 cups water in a deep bowl and marinate for at least 3 hours.

2. Preheat the oven to 350°F. Oil a baking sheet with a drizzle of olive oil.

3. Put the sweet potato and rutabaga in a large bowl and toss with the olive oil and 1½ teaspoons salt. Spread on the prepared baking sheet and roast for 15 to 25 minutes, or until soft. Remove from the oven and set aside, leaving the oven on.

4. Put the pistachios in a food processor and process until they have the consistency of bread crumbs. Pour onto a plate and set aside.

5. Lightly oil a second baking sheet. Remove the tofu slices from the marinade and lay them flat on the baking sheet. Sprinkle with a pinch of black pepper on both sides. Bake

RECIPE CONTINUES

for 3 to 5 minutes. Remove from the oven and carefully dredge the tofu slices in the crushed pistachios. Drizzle the baking sheet with olive oil and bake for 4 to 5 minutes more to toast the pistachios.

6. Meanwhile, in a small bowl, whisk together the vegan mayonnaise, truffle oil, lemon juice, remaining ½ teaspoon salt, remaining ½ teaspoon pepper, and ¼ cup water until well combined.

7. To assemble, divide the sauce between two plates, followed by the roasted vegetables, and top each with three triangles of tofu.

NOTE: This dish is best when you marinate the tofu for a few hours in advance, so plan ahead.

Eggplant is a staple of Middle Eastern cuisine. It is full of flavor, has a fantastic hearty texture, and is extremely versatile. Created as an inventive option for our gluten-free guests, this dish uses a combination of pine nuts and basil as the crust for the eggplant, and the creamy sauce is a wonderful finish. It's sure to please and impress at any dinner party and is great for all seasons.

PINE NUT–CRUSTED EGGPLANT

Serves 3 or 4

1 medium eggplant, halved and peeled

1½ tablespoons salt

3 medium Yukon Gold potatoes

2 cups pine nuts

1 cup all-purpose flour

1 cup plus 1 tablespoon chopped fresh basil

Scant ¾ cup olive oil

4½ tablespoons chopped garlic

1½ teaspoons salt, plus more as needed

3 pinches of black pepper

1 cup halved cherry tomatoes

1 sprig fresh rosemary, coarsely chopped

1 cup artichoke hearts

⅔ cup white wine

2 cups Cashew Cream (page 26)

1 head escarole

1. Preheat the oven to 350°F.

2. Slice the peeled eggplant lengthwise into ½-inch slices (each half should yield 6 slices). Fill a deep bowl with water and add 1 tablespoon of the salt. Soak the eggplant slices in the water for 20 minutes to help remove any bitterness.

3. Bring a pot of water to a boil and add the potatoes. Boil the potatoes for 30 to 40 minutes, or until soft, then remove and place in a large bowl.

4. While the potatoes are boiling and the eggplant is soaking, put the pine nuts, flour, and basil in a food processor. Process until the mixture has the consistency of bread crumbs. Transfer to a bowl and add 1½ tablespoons of the olive oil, 1½ tablespoons of the garlic, and a pinch each of salt and pepper. Mix well.

5. Drain the eggplant and dredge the slices in the pine nut breading, making sure each slice is thoroughly coated. Set the breaded eggplant slices on a rack and let sit for 10 to 20 minutes to dry.

RECIPE CONTINUES

6. Meanwhile, mash the potatoes with 2 tablespoons of the olive oil and 1 tablespoon of the garlic.

7. In a large skillet, heat 2 tablespoons of the olive oil over medium-high heat. Add 1 tablespoon of the garlic and sauté for 1 to 2 minutes. Add the tomatoes, rosemary, and artichoke hearts and sauté until the tomatoes begin to soften. Add ⅓ cup of the white wine and cook for 1 minute. Add the mashed potatoes and the salt and stir well.

8. In a large skillet, heat 3 tablespoons of the olive oil over medium heat. Add the eggplant slices and pan-fry on each side until they begin to lightly brown. Transfer to a baking sheet and bake for 3 to 5 minutes to crisp.

9. **Make the sauce:** In a large skillet, heat 2 tablespoons of the olive oil over medium-high heat. Add ½ tablespoon of the garlic and sauté for 1 to 2 minutes. Add the remaining ⅓ cup white wine, the Cashew Cream, and 1 tablespoon chopped basil and cook for 1 to 2 minutes. Add a pinch each of salt and pepper and stir.

10. In a separate medium skillet, heat the remaining 1 tablespoon olive oil over medium heat. Add the remaining ½ tablespoon garlic and sauté for 1 to 2 minutes, then add the escarole and sauté for 1 to 2 minutes, or until soft.

11. To assemble, divide the sauce among three or four plates, then add the potato mixture, the escarole, and finally the eggplant slices on top.

This is a wonderfully hearty entrée prepared with our favorite autumn produce—apples and butternut squash. The mouthwateringly rich, creamy polenta, combined with the sweetness of apples and tender cuts of seitan, make this dish one of our favorite fall dishes.

LEMON SEITAN
WITH CREAMY POLENTA

Serves 2

½ medium butternut squash, peeled, seeded, and diced

½ cup extra-virgin olive oil

3 tablespoons chopped fresh garlic

3 teaspoons salt, plus more as needed

1 cup all-purpose flour

6 palm-size slices of seitan, about ½ inch thick

2 tablespoons finely chopped shallot

½ cup sake

2 cups vegetable stock

1½ tablespoons fresh lemon juice

1 tablespoon vegan butter

1 tablespoon chopped scallion

1. Preheat the oven to 350°F.

2. Put the diced squash in a medium bowl and toss with 2 tablespoons of the olive oil, 1 tablespoon of the garlic, and a pinch of salt. Spread the squash on a baking sheet, cover with aluminum foil, and bake for 15 minutes, or until soft. Remove from the oven and set aside.

3. Put the flour in a medium bowl. Dredge the seitan cutlets in the flour until fully coated, then set aside.

4. In a medium skillet, heat 2 tablespoons of the olive oil over medium-high heat. Add the seitan cutlets and sauté, turning them periodically, for 3 minutes, until golden brown and crispy on both sides. Set aside.

5. Wipe out the skillet and heat 2 tablespoons of the olive oil over medium-high heat. Add 1 tablespoon of the shallots and sauté for 30 seconds, then add the seitan cutlets. Add the sake (be careful—it may flame a bit) and sauté for

RECIPE CONTINUES

1 tablespoon chopped fresh
parsley

1 cup diced unpeeled Granny
Smith apple

2 tablespoons white wine

Pinch of black pepper

1 cup polenta

1 minute. Add the stock, 2 teaspoons of the salt, the lemon juice, vegan butter, scallion, and parsley, and cook for about 2 minutes, or until the sauce begins to thicken.

6. In an oven-safe skillet, heat 2 tablespoons of the olive oil over medium heat. Add 1 tablespoon of the garlic, the roasted squash, apple, white wine, and a pinch each of salt and pepper. Transfer to the oven and bake for 2 to 3 minutes.

7. In a small pot, combine 3 cups water, the remaining 1 tablespoon chopped shallots, and remaining 1 tablespoon garlic and bring to a boil. Once boiling, add the polenta and cook, stirring continuously, until the water has been absorbed, about 3 minutes. Add the remaining 1 teaspoon salt and stir.

8. To assemble, divide the polenta between two plates, then plate the roasted apples and squash, and top with three seitan cutlets per serving. Cover with the pan sauce.

Our most classic: an original Blossom dish that has been my and Pamela's favorite from the start. Our customers agree—however, one in particular who comes to mind is Ted Danson. While he was in New York shooting a show for HBO, he came to Blossom almost daily for it. We serve our piccata with mashed potatoes and sautéed kale for a perfect all-season dish.

SEITAN PICCATA

Serves 4

5 medium potatoes (we use Yukon Gold), peeled

6 tablespoons vegan butter

1 tablespoon salt, plus more as needed

1½ teaspoons black pepper, plus more as needed

1½ pounds seitan

1 cup plus 3 tablespoons all-purpose flour

5 tablespoons extra-virgin olive oil

1 tablespoon chopped garlic

2 large bunches kale

¼ cup chopped fresh shallots

¾ cup white wine

¼ cup capers

Juice of 1 lemon

1 tablespoon chopped fresh parsley

1. Bring a large pot of water to boil and add the potatoes. Boil for 10 to 15 minutes, or until soft. Drain the potatoes and mash in a large bowl. Add 4 tablespoons of the vegan butter and season with salt and pepper. Cover and set aside.

2. Slice the seitan into palm-size cutlets (you should have 12 cutlets). Put 1 cup of the flour in a medium bowl and dredge the seitan in the flour, making sure to coat it thoroughly. Set aside.

3. In a large skillet, heat 2 tablespoons of the olive oil over medium-high heat. Add the seitan and sauté until browned and crispy on both sides. Set aside.

4. Wipe out the skillet and heat 1 tablespoon of the olive oil over medium-high heat. Add the garlic and sauté for 1 to 2 minutes. Add the kale and sauté for 3 to 4 minutes, or until soft. Add a pinch each of salt and pepper and set aside.

5. In a large sauté pan, heat the remaining 2 tablespoons olive oil over medium-high heat. Add the shallots and sauté

RECIPE CONTINUES

for 1 to 2 minutes, then add 2 tablespoons of the flour and stir well. Add the white wine (be careful—it may flame up), the capers, lemon juice, 1 tablespoon salt, 1½ teaspoons pepper, the parsley, the remaining 2 tablespoons vegan butter, and 4 cups water. Mix well and simmer the sauce for 1 to 2 minutes. Add the seitan cutlets to sauce and simmer for about 3 minutes, or until the sauce begins to the thicken.

6. To assemble, divide the mashed potatoes among four plates, followed by kale, and top each with three slices seitan. Finish with the pan sauce.

While we love being innovative and creating unique vegan dishes, we're also inspired by traditional ethnic dishes and love to reinvent our favorites with plant-based ingredients. We're not trying to imitate—we just want to capture the essence and feel of the original dish. And we always give it our own spin. Traditionally, cordon bleu is mostly meat and cheese, so it's not so easy to make a plant-based version, but we've done it! The result is deliciously satisfying.

SEITAN CORDON BLEU

Serves 4

4 medium-sized potatoes, peeled and roughly chopped

7 tablespoons vegan butter

2 tablespoons finely chopped garlic

2 tablespoons salt, plus 2 pinches

2 pinches of black pepper

1 pound seitan, approximately 8 palm-size slices about ¼ to ½ inch thick

½ (10-ounce) package vegan cheddar, thinly sliced

4 slices vegan ham

1 cup plus 1½ teaspoons all-purpose flour

1 cup soy milk

Leaves from 3 sprigs fresh thyme

1. Bring a large pot of water to a boil. Add potatoes and boil 10 to 15 minutes, or until soft. Drain water and mash. In a medium skillet on medium heat, add 5 tablespoons of the vegan butter and garlic, saute for 1 to 2 minutes, or until garlic begins to brown. Discard garlic and add infused vegan butter to potatoes along with 2 tablespoons salt and pepper. Set aside.

2. Thinly slice the seitan into approximately 8 palm-size pieces. Create 4 stacks by layering the seitan on the bottom, the cheese in the middle, slices of ham, followed by another layer of seitan on top.

3. In a medium bowl, combine 1 cup of the flour, the soy milk, thyme, and a pinch each of salt and pepper. Put 2 cups of the panko in a medium bowl. Dredge the stacks in the soy milk mixture first, followed by the panko. Coat very well and evenly. Set aside on a wire rack.

RECIPE CONTINUES

3 cups panko bread crumbs

4 tablespoons olive oil

1 tablespoon chopped shallot

1 cup sliced shiitake mushrooms

2/3 cup sake

1 cup cooking oil (we recommend grapeseed, safflower, or sunflower)

1½ teaspoons finely chopped garlic

3 handfuls collard greens

4. In a skillet, heat 2 tablespoons of the olive oil over high heat. Add the shallots and mushrooms and sauté for 1 to 2 minutes. Add the sake, remaining 1½ teaspoons flour, the butter, a pinch each of salt and pepper, and 1 cup water and cook for 5 to 10 minutes, until the sauce begins to reduce. Set aside.

5. In a deep skillet, heat the oil over medium-high heat. Add the seitan stacks and fry, flipping once, until golden brown, 2 to 3 minutes per side.

6. In a large sauté pan, heat the remaining 2 tablespoons olive oil over medium heat. Add the garlic and collard greens and sauté until soft.

7. To assemble, divide the mashed potatoes among four plates, followed by the collard greens and the cordon bleu stacks. Top with the shiitake sauce.

To me, a great chef must be creative. Chef Francisco concocts the most amazing dishes from ideas I bring to him. When I thought of reinventing my mother's stuffed peppers, for example, I asked Chef Francisco if he could find a way to make a refined, vegan version. The next day he invited me into the kitchen. To my joy, he had created a traditional Mexican *poblano en nogada*. This dish has a rich history in Mexico. In fact, the colors of the dish—the green of the poblanos, the white of the walnut sauce, and the red of the pomegranates—create the colors of the Mexican flag. The stuffing recipe has a rich umami quality without the traditional meat. It's great served with our cilantro rice on the side.

POBLANO EN NOGADA

Serves 4

4 large poblano peppers (as large as possible)

4 tablespoons olive oil

½ onion

2 cups finely minced seitan

2½ cups fresh or frozen diced peaches

1 red apple, peeled, cored, and diced (about 1½ cups)

⅓ cup raisins

2 tablespoons tomato paste

1½ teaspoons salt

Pinch of black pepper

1 cup soy milk

½ cup raw walnuts

1. Drizzle the poblanos with 2 tablespoons of the olive oil. Using long metal tongs, roast the peppers directly over the flame of a gas burner until the skins begin to bubble. Place in a large bowl and immediately cover the bowl with plastic wrap. Set aside to loosen the skins.

2. In a large pot, heat the remaining 2 tablespoons olive oil over high heat. Add the onion and sauté for 3 to 4 minutes. Add the seitan and sauté, stirring frequently, for 1 to 2 minutes. Add the peaches, apple, raisins, tomato paste, salt, pepper, and 4½ cups water. Reduce the heat to medium and cook, stirring frequently, until the liquid begins to reduce, 7 to 10 minutes.

3. Remove the poblanos from the bowl and use a kitchen towel to rub the peppers gently to remove the blackened skin (it should come off easily). Cut a slit down the side

RECIPE CONTINUES

½ cup raw almonds (preferably blanched)

1½ tablespoons apple cider vinegar

Pinch of ground cinnamon

½ cup pomegranate seeds (about ½ pomegranate)

of the pepper and carefully remove the seeds with your fingers, leaving the peppers as intact as possible. Set aside.

4. In a high-speed blender, blend the soy milk, walnuts, almonds, vinegar, and cinnamon until smooth.

5. To assemble, fill each pepper with the stuffing and drizzle with the sauce. Garnish with pomegranate seeds.

Chef Francisco loves to incorporate his Mexican heritage into Blossom's dishes. You can be assured that these enchiladas are authentic and are reminiscent of those found in the small villages of Mexico. The mole sauce, in combination with the mushroom in the enchiladas, jumps off the plate with spicy complexity. *¡Viva Mexican mole!*

ENCHILADAS

Serves 4

2 tablespoons extra-virgin olive oil

4 cups sliced shiitake mushrooms

½ medium fennel bulb, shaved on mandoline or thinly sliced

⅓ cup cooked corn

1½ teaspoons salt

8 corn or flour tortillas

3 cups Mole Sauce (page 32)

1 cup shredded vegan cheese

1 cup shredded lettuce

1 avocado, halved, pitted, and sliced

½ cup Sour Cream (page 27)

4 radishes, minced

1. Preheat the oven to 350°F.

2. In a large skillet, heat the olive oil over medium-high heat. Add the mushrooms, fennel, corn, and salt and sauté until the vegetables begin to brown. Portion the mixture out evenly between the tortillas, and gently roll them.

3. Place the rolled tortillas side by side on a rimmed baking sheet, cover with the Mole Sauce, and top with the vegan shredded cheese. Bake until the cheese just melts fully, 3 to 5 minutes. Remove from the oven, and serve topped with lettuce, avocado, Sour Cream, and radishes.

Paella: Spain's most beloved, traditional, and famous dish. Rather than doing a traditional rice and vegetable dish, we wanted to make an all-vegetable paella. We swapped the rice with mashed cauliflower and added a phenomenal combination of vegetables and saffron, giving the dish both incredible exotic flavor as well as this entrée's beautiful yellow hue. A truly healthful dish that doesn't compromise on taste. It works just as well as a side dish or a starter. *¡Olé!*

CAULIFLOWER PAELLA

Serves 2

1 medium head cauliflower

2 tablespoons olive oil

½ medium onion, finely chopped

1 large tomato or 2 or 3 small plum tomatoes, diced

½ pound oyster mushrooms (roughly 12 mushrooms)

3 large artichoke hearts, quartered (remove stem if necessary)

1 red bell pepper, julienned

½ teaspoon saffron

½ cup fresh green peas (or frozen, if that's what you have on hand)

½ cup green olives, chopped or whole

1 tablespoon salt

1 teaspoon black pepper

1. Remove the stem from the cauliflower, discard and chop the head roughly. Place the cauliflower in a food processor and pulse seven or eight times, or until it is finely minced, similar to the size and consistency of grains of rice.

2. In a large pot, heat the olive oil over medium-high heat. Add the onion, raise the heat to high, and sauté for 2 to 3 minutes, or until transparent. Add the tomato and sauté for 2 to 3 minutes. Add the mushrooms, artichoke hearts, and bell peppers and sauté for 1 to 2 minutes. Add the cauliflower and stir well to combine, then add 3 cups water. Bring the mixture to a boil, then reduce the heat to medium. Add the saffron, peas, olives, salt, and black pepper and simmer until the water has been absorbed, 4 to 5 minutes.

DESSERTS

The "key" to this dish is the fresh lime juice—accept no substitutions! You won't believe the fantastic texture of this pie—the avocados add an unbelievable creaminess to the filling. This recipe comes from Quinn, Blossom's fantastic baker-in-chief.

RAW KEY LIME PIE

Makes one 9-inch pie

FOR THE CRUST

1¼ cups macadamia nuts

1¼ cups pecans

½ cup dried, pitted dates, soaked in water for 1 hour

Pinch of salt

¼ teaspoon vanilla extract

FOR THE FILLING

1½ cups fresh lime juice (from about 12 limes)

1 cup agave syrup

½ cup full-fat coconut milk

2 ripe avocados, halved, pitted, and peeled

2 tablespoons vanilla extract

¼ teaspoon salt

1¼ cups coconut oil

1. Make the crust: Lightly grease a 9-inch springform baking pan with coconut oil.

2. Put the macadamia nuts, pecans, dates, salt, and vanilla in a food processor and process until the mixture is soft and easily workable. Press the mixture into the bottom of the prepared pan.

3. Make the filling: Put the lime juice, agave, coconut milk, avocados, vanilla, salt, and coconut oil in a high-speed blender and blend until smooth.

4. Pour the filling over the crust, cover with plastic wrap, and freeze overnight. Thaw before serving.

This light dessert is perfect for airy summer nights when fresh peaches are in season! Delicious served hot or cold, it's even better with a scoop of soy or coconut ice cream on top.

PEACH COBBLER

Serves 4

FOR THE PEACH FILLING

½ cup sugar or agave syrup

4 cups sliced fresh peaches

¼ cup brandy

1 tablespoon vanilla extract

FOR THE CRUMBLE

5 ounces vegan vanilla snap cookies

½ cup coconut flakes

2 tablespoons vegan butter

Vanilla ice cream, for serving

1. Preheat the oven to 350°F.

2. **Make the peach filling:** In a medium saucepan, heat the sugar over medium heat for about 1 minute. Stir in the peaches, brandy, and vanilla. Reduce the heat to medium and cook for 3 to 4 minutes. Remove from the heat and set aside.

3. **Make the crumble:** Put the cookies in a food processor and process into crumbs. Add the coconut flakes and the vegan butter and process for 30 seconds.

4. Divide the peach filling among four individual small ramekins, miniature cast-iron pans, or other oven-safe dishes and top evenly with the crumble. Gently press the crumble down with your hands. Bake for 2 to 3 minutes, or until the crumble begins to brown slightly. Top with vanilla ice cream and serve!

If you want a more elegant and stylish take on a classic apple pie, try our Phyllo Apple Sticks. When I was growing up, many of my favorite dishes contained phyllo, so this is a particular favorite of mine. In this delightful dessert, the brandy sauce really brings everything together, but a scoop of soy, almond, or coconut ice cream finishes it with pure bliss! When apple season comes around in the fall, you're sure to find us making this recipe, and we hope you do, too.

PHYLLO APPLE STICKS IN BRANDY SAUCE

Serves 4

FOR THE APPLE STICKS

3 Granny Smith apples, peeled, cored, and chopped into ½-inch cubes

½ cup packed brown sugar

⅓ cup brandy

½ teaspoon ground cinnamon

1 teaspoon vanilla extract

4 large sheets phyllo

3 tablespoons vegan butter, melted

1. Make the apple sticks: In a medium pot, heat the brown sugar over high heat, stirring continuously, for about 3 minutes. Stir in the apples and the brandy and cook for about 2 minutes. Add the cinnamon and vanilla, stir, and remove from the heat.

2. Stack the phyllo sheets. Using a pastry brush, spread melted vegan butter on top of the stacked phyllo sheets. Spread half of the apple mixture along one long side of the phyllo, ½ to 1 inch away from the edge. Starting from the edge with the filling, roll up the phyllo into a tight cylinder, making sure not to break the phyllo (it can be very delicate). Once it is rolled, cut it crosswise into eight equal sections. Repeat these steps to create another phyllo roll.

3. In a medium skillet, heat the remaining melted vegan butter over medium heat. Add the apple phyllo sticks and cook, turning frequently, until crisp and golden.

RECIPE CONTINUES

FOR THE BRANDY SAUCE

½ cup granulated sugar

½ cup brandy

1 cup soy milk

1 cup coconut milk

1 teaspoon vanilla extract

Fresh strawberries, for serving

Confectioners' sugar, for garnish (optional)

4. **Make the brandy sauce:** In a medium saucepan, heat the sugar over high heat, while stirring, for about 1 minute. Add the brandy (be cautious of flames), cook for about 30 seconds, then add the soy milk, coconut milk, and vanilla and stir well. Bring the mixture to a boil, then reduce the heat to medium and simmer for 3 to 4 minutes. Let cool slightly before serving.

5. To serve, top the apple sticks with brandy sauce and fresh strawberries. Garnish with a dusting of confectioners' sugar, if desired.

Believe it or not, German chocolate cake isn't from Germany at all—it was invented by a baker named Samuel German back in the nineteenth century! We took it to the next level by veganizing it. After all, the main elements—chocolate, coconut, and pecans—are naturally vegan. This chocolatey delight comes from Quinn, our baker extraordinaire.

GERMAN CHOCOLATE CAKE

Makes one 9-inch, three-layer cake

FOR THE CHOCOLATE CAKE

3 cups all-purpose flour

3¼ cups sugar

1 cup unsweetened cocoa powder

1 tablespoon baking soda

½ teaspoon salt

3 cups soy milk

1 tablespoon apple cider vinegar

1 cup grapeseed, safflower, or sunflower oil

2 tablespoons vanilla extract

1. Preheat the oven to 350°F. Grease three 9-inch-diameter cake pans with a thin layer of coconut oil.

2. Make the chocolate cake: In a large bowl, combine the flour, sugar, cocoa powder, baking soda, and salt. Mix well. Add the soy milk and vinegar and let curdle for a moment to create a vegan buttermilk. Add the oil and vanilla. Whisk until well combined. Pour the mixture evenly among the prepared pans. Bake for 20 minutes. Feel free to check for doneness by sticking a clean toothpick into the center of each cake—it will come out clean if done (the cake should also "spring back" to the touch). Remove from the oven and let cool in the pan on a wire rack.

3. After the cakes have cooled, remove the cakes from the pans, and cut off the domed tops to make a flat, level surface. Set aside.

4. Make the filling/topping: In a small bowl, whisk together the cornstarch and 5 tablespoons water.

RECIPE CONTINUES

FOR THE FILLING/TOPPING

5 tablespoons cornstarch

1 (16-ounce) can coconut milk

1½ cups agave syrup

½ cup vegan butter

1 tablespoon vanilla extract

5 cups dried, shredded, unsweetened coconut

1½ cups chopped pecans

5. In a medium saucepan, whisk together the coconut milk, agave, vegan butter, and vanilla and bring to a boil over high heat. Pour a small amount of the hot coconut liquid into the cornstarch slurry, while continuously whisking. Then, add the cornstarch mixture back into the original pan, while whisking continuously. This is called tempering. Let the mixture return to a boil—the liquid will thicken as it cooks. Turn off the heat and gently stir in the shredded coconut and pecans.

6. To assemble: Set one cake layer on a cake platter or serving plate. Spread one-third of the filling over the layer. Set a second layer on top and spread one-third of the filling over the layer. Top with the final cake layer and spread the remaining filling over the top.

You'd never guess this classic lemon–poppy seed cake was vegan, let alone gluten-free! Brown rice flour, garbanzo bean flour, and potato starch take the place of traditional wheat flour in this recipe. We like to coat the sides of the cake in poppy seeds as well for a striking presentation. This is another wonderfully creative sweet from Quinn, Blossom's expert baker.

GLUTEN-FREE LEMON POPPY CAKE

Makes one 9-inch two-layer cake

FOR THE LEMON CAKE

3 cups brown rice flour

2½ cups garbanzo bean flour

1 cup potato starch

½ cup arrowroot powder

1 to 2 cups poppy seeds
   (depending on garnish)

2 tablespoons baking powder

1½ teaspoons baking soda

1½ teaspoons xanthan gum

1 tablespoon kosher salt

1½ cups agave syrup

1½ cups unsweetened
   applesauce

1¼ cups coconut oil

1 tablespoon vanilla extract

1 tablespoon lemon oil extract

1. **Make the lemon cake:** Preheat the oven to 350°F. Grease and lightly flour two 9-inch cake pans with a thin layer of coconut oil.

2. In a large bowl, whisk together the brown rice flour, garbanzo bean flour, potato starch, arrowroot powder, poppy seeds, baking powder, baking soda, xanthan gum, and salt until well combined. While whisking, in this order, add the agave, applesauce, coconut oil, vanilla, lemon extract, and 1 cup water. Whisk until smooth.

3. Divide the batter evenly between the prepared pans. Bake for 40 to 50 minutes. Check for doneness by sticking a clean toothpick into the center of each cake—it will come out clean if done (the cake should also "spring back" to the touch). Remove from the oven and let cool in the pans on a wire rack.

4. **Make the frosting:** While the cake is baking, in the bowl of a stand mixer fitted with the paddle attachment, beat the vegan butter, vegan cream cheese, vanilla, lemon oil, and

RECIPE CONTINUES

FOR THE LEMON CREAM CHEESE FROSTING

¾ cup vegan butter

¾ cup vegan cream cheese

1 tablespoon vanilla extract

¼ teaspoon lemon oil extract

Pinch of salt

3⅓ cups organic confectioners' sugar, sifted

Poppy seeds, for garnish (optional)

salt until smooth. (If you don't have a stand mixer, let the butter soften to room temperature and blend by hand using a spatula.) Add the sifted powdered sugar to the mixture slowly, until the consistency has reached desired stiffness.

5. **To assemble:** Remove the finished cakes from the pans. Set one cake layer on a cake platter or serving plate. Spread a ½-inch-thick layer of the filling over the cake. Top with the second cake layer, then frost the entire cake, including the sides. If desired, gently coat the outside of the cake with poppy seeds (place the finished cake on a large sheet pan and, using your hands, gently coat the sides of the cake with poppy seeds).

ACKNOWLEDGMENTS

"It takes a village." No other adage could be truer when creating a successful restaurant. We would be remiss if we did not acknowledge and express our deep gratitude to the many wonderful people along the way who have helped us make Blossom what it is today. Without this dedicated group, Blossom would have remained only a dream, and never grown into what it is— a pioneer in cruelty-free food, proudly proving to the world, one delicious meal at a time, that animal-free cuisine is every bit as flavorful, decadent, and varied as any other.

From our original location at our cozy two-story historic town house in Chelsea, to our spacious and elegant location on the Upper West Side, and our in-demand catering business, we have been honored to take this journey with so many caring and passionate people, both in the front of house staff as well as the back of house staff, all of whom have brought their love of animals and for fantastic food with them to Blossom every day. Mostly notably, Chef Francisco, for his incredible creativity and tireless work ethic, pushing us all to the next level of excellence on a daily basis. To our indispensable general manager at our Chelsea location, Michael Parkin, for his dedication, experience, and for making the very intense day-to-day operations seem so easy and seamless.

We'd like to thank everyone at Avery and Penguin Random House, particularly Lucia Watson, our editor, and Nina Caldas, our editorial assistant, for their constant support and guidance through a process that was very much uncharted territory for us. Much appreciation goes to our agent, Meg Thompson of Thompson Literary Agency, who saw the bright future of *The Blossom Cookbook* early on. To the Erickson Family and Seventh House PR, who inspired us to share Blossom's vision and food with the public at large. And to Alex Etling, our photographer, copywriter, and media guru, who truly brings our food to life both visually and verbally. We owe Alex and Sara Rotter great thanks for their creative and technical input in the writing of this book. On a personal note, Pamela and I would like to express appreciation for the constant and unyielding love and support of friends and family.

Most of all, we are so grateful to our guests who have joined us for lunch, brunch, or dinner over the years, many of whom have become cherished regulars. We couldn't have done it without your enthusiastic support, and we look forward to many more years of serving you the best vegan cuisine out there!

ABOUT THE AUTHORS

Born in Jerusalem, Israel, **RONEN SERI** moved to New York City to pursue a career in acting. A born entrepreneur, Ronen funded his passion for acting by opening a variety of successful businesses that sustained his creative pursuits. A self-proclaimed foodie, Ronen opened Blossom's flagship restaurant in Chelsea in 2005 with the hope of redefining the art of vegan cooking and elevating it as a popular cuisine in and of itself. While he spends much of his time and energy researching, exploring, and curating exciting dishes for the restaurant, you can also follow his YouTube "how to" cooking series. In the fall of 2016, he opened an all-vegan ice cream, crepe, and Belgium waffle eatery called Gela, located in the busiest market in Jerusalem. In his spare time, Ronen enjoys traveling the world and meditation. More recently, he has found a great amount of joy through writing, and as such, has been working on a fiction novel as well as a stage play, to be produced.

PAMELA ELIZABETH is a New York City native and has been a passionate vegan for more than twenty years. She ultimately realized that serving vegan food to the public was the most effective form of activism. Through her endeavors of Blossom Restaurant, Blossom du Jour, and Urban Vegan Kitchen, her goal is to spread awareness of animal oppression and ultimately promote a cruelty-free lifestyle. Elizabeth is an avid cook, recipe developer, photographer, opera singer, and animal lover.

Chef **RAMIRO RAMIREZ** has been a valued member of the Blossom family since 2007, and is responsible for many of the delicious creations that have put Blossom on the culinary map. He was vital to the opening and managing of two of our locations, and was responsible for assembling and training Blossom's expert kitchen team. Before joining us, Chef Ramiro trained under the supervision of top chefs at some of New York City's most prestigious restaurants, but he found his gift for creating incredible vegan dishes here at Blossom.

ALEX ETLING, photographer | A.Etling Photography. An ethical vegan since 2008, Alex feels tremendously lucky to be a part of the Blossom family, where he is able to indulge his love for photography, delicious vegan food, and the wonderful synthesis of the two. Alex is also a professional actor, and co-founder and managing director of Cave Theatre Co. in New York City, one of his proudest artistic endeavors. He currently lives on the Upper West Side of Manhattan with his fiancée, Kiley, and their awesome dog, Olive. If you'd like to see more of Alex's photography, go to aetlingphoto.com or follow him on Instagram at @aetlingphoto.

INDEX